A NEW OWNER'S
GUIDE TO
ROTTWEILERS

JG-101

Overleaf: Adult and puppy Rottweilers owned by the Lubrichs.

Opposite Page: The nobility of the Rottweiler is evident in its expression.

The Publisher wishes to acknowledge the following owners of the dogs in this book: Bill Alexander, Kathy L, Allen, Canil Baruki's, Suzanne E. Burris, George S. Chamberlin, Eddy Choong, Amy Creteau, John Erbert, Diana D. Gibson, Ron Gibson, Pamela Grant, Nancy Griego, L. Herring, Arthur Israel, Robben Jones, Rod and Eric Kerr, Linda Latham, Harold Litte, The Lubrichs, Marrian McShane, Deborah Moregue, Nance Reynolds, Lori Rizzitano, D. & B. Rollins, Robert C. Sarro, Catherine M. Thompson, LaCinda Toller and Dr. Margaret Zazzaro.

Photographers: Mary Bloom, Paulette Braun, Isabelle Francais, Urs Ochsenbein, Robert Pearcy, Ron Reagan, Vince Serbin, Robert Smith, Judith Strom and Karen Taylor. Original art by John Quinn.

The author acknowledges the contribution of: Judy Iby for the following chapters: Behavior and Canine Communication, Traveling with Your Dog, Identification and Finding the Lost Dog, Sport of Purebred Dogs and Health Care.

Translated by Holger Homann.

Distributed in the UNITED STATES to the Pet Trade by T.F.H. Publications, Inc., One T.F.H. Plaza, Neptune City, NJ 07753; distributed in the UNITED STATES to the Bookstore and Library Trade by National Book Network, Inc. 4720 Boston Way, Lanham MD 20706; in CANADA to the Pet Trade by H & L Pet Supplies Inc., 27 Kingston Crescent, Kitchener, Ontario N2B 2T6; Rolf C. Hagen Inc., 3225 Sartelon St. Laurent-Montreal Quebec H4R 1E8; in CANADA to the Book Trade by Vanwell Publishing Ltd., 1 Northrup Crescent, St. Catharines, Ontario L2M 6P5 ; in ENGLAND by T.F.H. Publications, PO Box 15, Waterlooville PO7 6BQ; in AUSTRA-LIA AND THE SOUTH PACIFIC by T.F.H. (Australia), Pty. Ltd., Box 149, Brookvale 2100 N.S.W., Australia; in NEW ZEALAND by Brooklands Aquarium Ltd. 5 McGiven Drive, New Plymouth, RD1 New Zealand; in Japan by T.F.H. Publications, Japan— Jiro Tsuda, 10-12-3 Ohjidai, Sakura, Chiba 285, Japan; in SOUTH AFRICA by Lopis (Pty) Ltd., P.O. Box 39127, Booysens, 2016, Johannesburg, South Africa. Published by T.F.H. Publications, Inc.

MANUFACTURED IN THE
UNITED STATES OF AMERICA
BY T.F.H. PUBLICATIONS, INC.

A New Owner's
Guide to
Rottweilers

Urs Ochsenbein

Contents

Feed your Rottweiler puppy what he is accustomed to.

A Rottweiler is very trusting of his human partner.

Rottweiler puppies are irresistible.

The German word "Schutzhund" means "Protection Dog" in English.

The Rottweiler is a dog of compact and yet substantial build.

INTRODUCTION to the Rottweiler

The Rottweiler stands out from the many other breeds of dog that exist because of his massive shape, which has not changed since he came into existence. He displays neither an overly long coat that covers the eyes, nor skin with extreme folds, nor varied coloration, nor an excessively heavy skull. He is powerfully and harmoniously built and appears massive but is nevertheless agile. The proportion of head to body is normal. The ears suit his general appearance without cropping. The Rottweiler is no attractive dazzler but rather a dignified dog of rustic appearance.

There are many reasons to recommend the Rottweiler. He is big, beautiful and sure to attract attention wherever you take him.

It is this delight over the natural form and character of this breed that attracts fanciers to the Rottweiler. People who want to be noticed will surely not buy a dog with no great oddities about him. Perhaps there are a few people who have heard of the Rottweiler's strength, determination, and courage and acquire one with the intent of owning an aggressive defender; however, here, the Rottweiler would be in the wrong hands. This breed is fundamentally good natured and even tempered and not all that easily irritated. Those who force him into their ideal of a "bad dog" and apply the necessary ruthlessness will indeed come into a dangerous animal. By then we are dealing with a ruined Rottweiler who is no longer at peace with himself; we are dealing with a dog who has been made insecure by the bad experiences with his master and his master's accomplices and who directs all his strength and quickness into aggression that no longer can be controlled. The same thing, unfortunately, also happens again and again to dogs from other working breeds.

The recipe for making a Rottweiler into a good and reliable guardian and protector is so very simple: make sure that he feels comfortable in his home territory. Sooner or later, he will, all by himself, assume responsibility for the safety of the house and its inhabitants; it is part and parcel of his natural protective behavior. Sure, we must be willing to wait out his development. In this regard he numbers among the late-maturing dogs and it takes time for him to become an adult in mind and body. Those who demand aggressive behavior of him before he is ready, ask too much of him. Such a Rottweiler, once he has grown up, will in all likelihood be difficult to control. After all, he is by nature a bold fellow, and one should not attempt to instill this trait into him artificially.

Schutzhund training involves three facets: tracking, obedience (including retrieving), and protection.

For Whom and What Purpose Is the Rottweiler Appropriate?

A Rottweiler, prudently bred and

expertly raised from puppyhood, is very adaptable. He is suitable as a simple family dog and companion and can also be used in all areas of dog sports. He proves his value as a utility dog by working with the police, the military, the custom service, and as a rescue dog. He even serves reliably as a Seeing Eye™ dog. For all these tasks, however, there are two prerequisites.

One, the Rottweiler is a sensitive and bright animal that will waste away if we pay him too little attention and leave him to himself without anything to do. This is basically true for all dogs.

Two, the Rottweiler needs a firm hand since otherwise he may become independent and get out of control due to his innate hard temperament and his physical strength. A "firm hand," however,

A Rottweiler is a sensitive breed that requires love, attention, a firm hand and proper training.

does not mean in any way that this dog should be dominated by brute force. Rather, it means making him consistently aware, from puppyhood on, of what he may and may not do. Then he will become an enjoyable, pleasant, and useful member of the family.

ORIGIN OF THE ROTTWEILER

Some breed clubs, carried away by their enthusiasm for their breed, ascribe to their dogs an imaginary glorious past, adducing recklessly and without justification terms such as "molossus" and "fighting dog" in the process. In his Rottweiler book, Adolf Pienko says the following regarding this topic: *"All published statements on the true ancestors of the Rottweiler are based on assertions that cannot be substantiated through sound scientific research."* This statement is true for all breeds known today unless they have been created at some time during the past one hundred years. Much has been asserted but little proven in regard to the origins of the various dog breeds. Thus let us stick to what is really known.

Our Rottweiler, in particular, does not need for us to engage in ancestor worship. But there does exist a guild sign dated 1886 that shows a butcher and an ox who is being nipped on the fetlock by a typical Rottweiler. At that time, many of the breeds recognized today did not yet exist. Thus we are justified in referring to the Rottweiler as an "old breed."

Droving comes naturally to the Rottweiler; most of today's specimens will immediately perform when given the opportunity to drive cattle. For centuries Rottweilers have been kept as working dogs by butchers and farmers who needed them for moving their herds. Unlike today, in those times cattle had to be brought to the consumer live and that

The Rottweiler's great strength comes from his heritage as a draft dog. Legend says that Roman soldiers used the breed to drive and guard the stock.

frequently meant weeks of droving work. This was almost impossible to do without suitable dogs. Obviously, only the best dogs survived this labor; weaker animals were eliminated by their owners. Thus a selection took place—the positive effects of which are still visible today in the Rottweiler's generally confident behavior and temperament.

If we want to go back even further, we are reduced to making assumptions. We may assume with a fair degree of probability that the Rottweiler is a descendant—as are other typical cattle dogs, such as the Boxer—of the *Bullenbeisser*, of whom there exist authentic pictures. The *Bullenbeisser*, in turn, seems to come from those

Nearly 2000 years ago Roman soldiers brought to the town of Rottweil their dogs of war...today's Rottweiler.

mastiff-like dogs that were used for hunting boar and bear in the days when these animals were not shot with guns but killed with spears. Only dogs with pronounced boldness were suitable for this kind of hunt. We still find clear traces of this kind of temperament in today's Rottweiler.

The town of Rottweil that gave our breed its name, lies at the crossroads of old trade routes that, in part, were established by the ancient Romans. Along these very routes, herds of cattle were driven to faraway towns. It is only natural that the professionals who made this kind of trek should have bred the most suitable dog as their assistant and protector—the Rottweiler.

STANDARD for the Rottweiler

So that all breeders of a given breed may strive toward a common breeding goal in regard to the outward appearance of the breed type involved, a precise description of what is thought to be the ideal type is established. This description is called the standard. Of course, interested friends of the breed and their breed councils frequently differ in their opinions and a standard must be arrived at through negotiations. The first Rottweiler standard came into being as early as 1901. After that, a number of revised versions were published. This is quite understandable since breeds arc continuously evolving. Furthermore, whatever is chosen as the ideal type at one time is subject to continuous revision since the opinions and conceptions held by the people involved with the breed change. Thus, we must always expect small adjustments.

By reading this standard, Rottweiler owners can find out which outward appearance and which anatomical characteristics are desired and to what extent all this

The Rottweiler should possess a fearless expression that does not lend itself to immediate and indiscriminate friendships.

applies to one's own dog. This, however, cannot take the place of an expert's counsel and evaluation, preferably that of a judge at a show or match. Only then will we know where our dog stands.

THE AMERICAN KENNEL CLUB STANDARD FOR THE ROTTWEILER

General Appearance: The ideal Rottweiler is a medium large, robust and powerful dog, black with clearly defined rust markings. His compact and substantial build denotes great strength, agility and endurance. Dogs are characteristically more massive throughout with larger frame and heavier bone than bitches. Bitches are distinctly feminine, but without weakness of substance or structure.

Size, Proportion, Substance: Dogs—24 inches to 27 inches. Bitches—22 inches to 25 inches,

The Rottweiler's compact and substantial build denotes great strength, agility and endurance.

with preferred size being mid-range of each sex. Correct proportion is of primary importance, as long as size is within the standard's range. The length of body, from prosternum to the rearmost projection of the rump, is slightly longer than the height to length being 9 to 10. The Rottweiler is neither coarse nor shelly. Depth of chest is approximately 50 percent of the dog. His bone and muscle mass must be sufficient to balance his frame, giving a compact and very powerful appearance. *Serious Faults:* Lack of proportion, undersized, oversized, reversal of sex characteristics (bitchy dogs, doggy bitches).

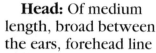

Rust markings on the Rottweiler's head should be clearly defined and properly located—a spot above each eye, on the cheeks, and a strip around each side of the muzzle.

Head: Of medium length, broad between the ears, forehead line seen in profile is moderately arched, zygomatic arch and stop well developed with strong broad upper and lower jaws. The desired ratio of backskull to muzzle is 3 to 2. Forehead is preferred dry, however some wrinkling may occur when dog is alert. *Expression* is noble, alert, and self-assured. Eyes of medium size, almond shaped with well fitting lids, moderately deep-set, neither protruding nor receding. The desired color is a uniform dark brown. *Serious Faults:* Yellow (bird of prey) eyes, eyes of different color or size, hairless eye rim. *Disqualification:* Entropion. Ectropion. **Ears:** Of medium size, pendant, triangular in shape; when carried alertly the ears are level with the top of the skull and appear to broaden it. Ears are to be set well apart; hanging forward with the inner edge lying tightly against

A Rottweiler puppy will be a miniature version of his adult parents. This is why good breeding is essential to producing good offspring.

the head and terminating at approximately mid-cheek. **Serious Faults:** Improper carriage (creased, folded or held away from cheek/head).

Muzzle: Bridge is straight, broad at base and slight tapering toward tip. The end of the muzzle is broad with well developed chin. Nose is broad rather than round and always black. **Lips:** Always black; corners closed; inner mouth pigment is preferred dark. **Serious Faults:** Total lack of mouth pigment (pink mouth). **Bite and Dentition:** Teeth 42 in number (20 upper, 22 lower), strong, correctly placed, meeting in a scissors bite—lower incisors touching inside of upper incisors. **Serious Faults:** Level bite; any missing tooth. **Disqualifications:** Overshot, undershot (when incisors do not touch or mesh); wry mouth; two or more missing teeth.

Neck, Topline, Body: *Neck:* Powerful, well muscled, moderately long, slightly arched and without loose skin. *Topline:* The back is firm and level, extending in a straight line from behind the withers to the croup. The back remains horizontal to the ground while the dog is moving or standing. *Body:* The chest is roomy, broad and deep, reaching to elbow, with well pronounced forechest and well sprung, oval ribs. Back is straight and strong. Loin is short, deep and well muscled. Croup is broad, of medium length and only slightly sloping. Underline of a mature Rottweiler has a slight tuck-

A Rottweiler's power not only lies in his body structure but in his movement as well. It is easy to see how this breed excels in activities such as obedience and agility.

up. Males must have two normal testicles properly descended into the scrotum. ***Disqualification***: Unilateral cryptorchid or cryptorchid males. ***Tail***: Tail docked short, close to body, leaving one or two tail vertebrae. The set of the tail is more important than length. Properly set, it gives an impression of elongation of topline, carried slightly above horizontal when the dog is excited or moving.

Forequarters: Shoulder blade is long and well laid back. Upper arm equal in length to shoulder blade, set so elbows are well under body. Distance from withers to elbow and elbow to ground is equal. Legs are strongly developed with straight, heavy bone, not set close together. Pasterns are strong, springy and almost perpendicular to the ground. Feet are round, compact with well arched toes, turning neither in nor out. Pads are thick and hard. Nails short, strong, and black. Dewclaws may be removed.

The upper arm of the Rottweiler is equal in length to the shoulder blade and set so the elbows are well under, or over (as the case may be), the body.

Hindquarters: Angulation of hindquarters balances that of forequarters. Upper thigh is fairly long, very broad and well muscled. Stifle joint is well turned. Lower thigh is long, broad and powerful, with extensive muscling leading into a strong hock joint. Rear pasterns are nearly perpendicular to the ground. Viewed from the rear, hind legs are straight, strong and wide enough apart to fit with a properly built body. Feet are somewhat longer than the front feet, turning neither in nor out, equally compact with well arched toes. Pads are thick and hard. Nails short, strong, and black. Dewclaws must be removed.

Coat: Outer coat is straight, coarse, dense, of medium length and lying flat. Undercoat should be present on neck and thighs, but the amount is influenced by climate conditions. Undercoat should not show through outer coat. The coat is shortest on head, ears and legs, longest on breeching. The Rottweiler is to be exhibited in the natural condition with no trimming. *Fault*: Wavy coat. *Serious Faults*: Open excessively short, or curly coat, total lack of undercoat; any trimming that alters the length of the natural coat. *Disqualification*: Long coat.

Color: Always black with rust to mahogany markings. The demarcation between black and rust is to be clearly defined. The markings should be located as follows: a spot over each eye; on cheeks; as a strip around each side of muzzle, but not on the bridge of the nose; on throat; triangular mark on both sides of prosternum; on forelegs from carpus downward to the toes; on inside of rear legs showing down the front of the stifle and broadening out to front of rear legs from hocks to toes, but not completely eliminating black from rear of pasterns; under tail, black penciling on toes. The undercoat is gray, tan, or black. Quantity and location of rust markings is important and should not exceed ten percent of body color. *Serious Faults*: Straw-colored, excessive, insufficient or sooty markings; rust marking other than described above; white marking any place on dog (a few rust or white hairs do not constitute a marking).
Disqualifications: Any base color other than black, absence of all markings.

Gait: The Rottweiler is a trotter. His movement should be balanced, harmonious, sure, powerful and unhindered, with strong forereach and a powerful rear drive. The motion is effortless, efficient, and ground-covering. Front and rear legs are thrown neither in nor out, as the imprint of hind feet should touch that of forefeet. In a trot the forequarters and hindquarters are mutually coordinated while the back remains level, firm and relatively motionless. As speed increases the legs will converge under body towards a center line.

Temperament: The Rottweiler is basically a calm, confident and courageous dog with a self-assured aloofness that does not lend itself to immediate and indiscriminate friendships. A Rottweiler is self-confident and responds quietly and with a wait-and-see attitude to influences in his environment. He has an inherent desire to protect home and family, and is an intelligent dog of extreme hardness and adaptability with a strong willingness to work, making him especially suited as a companion, guardian and general all-purpose dog.

The Rottweiler will generally adore your children but caution and common sense should always be followed when dealing with a dog of this size.

The behavior of the Rottweiler in the show ring should be controlled, willing, adaptable, trained to submit to examination of mouth, testicles, etc. An aloof or reserved dog should not be penalized, as this reflects the accepted character of the breed. An aggressive or belligerent attitude towards other dogs should not be faulted.

A judge shall excuse from the ring any shy Rottweiler. A dog shall be judged fundamentally shy if, refusing to stand for examination, it shrinks away from the judge.

A dog that in the opinion of the judge menaces or threatens him/her, or exhibits any sign that it may not be safely approached or examined by the judge in the normal manner, shall be excused from the ring. A dog that in the opinion of the judge attacks any person in the ring shall be disqualified.

BUYING a Rottweiler

A Rottweiler brings with him responsibility for his care and training. After all, he is not a toy that we stash in a corner after we are through with him. He is always there and demands that we pay him attention. With a young Rottweiler, this happens in most cases spontaneously. Several times a day he will feel an urgent need for affection, for play and interaction. If we were to constantly reject him, he will look for ways to entertain himself. He will begin by working on anything that offers itself to be worked on.

When purchasing your Rottweiler, keep in mind that you don't have to purchase a puppy. You can obtain a full-grown, well-trained adult.

Carpets and furniture are no more safe from him than are the wastepaper baskets and curtains. Whatever bad habits he acquires at this time, which later we may find difficult to correct, will be our own fault since we were not willing to involve ourselves with him.

Later, when the dog has grown older, we can direct his need for affection into a routine and build it into the daily activities of the family. But this does not work with a young dog of 12 months or less. Nevertheless, even with a puppy we will have "rest periods" of one to two hours when he recovers from his most recent experiences. Those quarter or half hours when he looks for us offer the best opportunity to learn with him in play and, at the same time, to establish a deep and satisfying relationship with him. Thus it would be a pity if we could not or would not involve ourselves with our young Rottweiler whenever he asks it of us. Sure, it is possible to lock the dog into a crate where he cannot cause any damage and where he is left to entertain himself with some toys we throw in with him. In this scenario, we deprive our dog of what he needs most:

contact with people. Everyone must decide for himself, if and to what extent, he plans to involve himself with the developing animal. It will require time, but it is also fun and serves to integrate the dog into the family.

Keep in mind that high-spirited dogs—and this usually includes the Rottweiler—will be more demanding in the beginning than more placid dogs. That is a point to consider when choosing our puppy. After all this, it should be clear that a young Rottweiler will require our attention several times a day. Further, we should plan on one and a half hours a day for two separate walks, if possible, in areas where encounters with other dogs are likely. If we are willing and able to spend this amount of time with our dog, one of the most important prerequisites for proper dog ownership is fulfilled. After all, dogs, including the Rottweiler, are animals with a great need for exercise.

Simple training, such as teaching your Rottweiler his name or how to walk on a leash, is done when the puppy is eight to ten weeks of age.

There are a few more questions that should be answered before we acquire a dog:

1. Does the lease for our apartment allow a dog? It happens again and again that dogs must be given away because the landlord won't allow dogs.

2. Is there a family member who suffers from allergic reactions to dog hair? This would preclude owning a dog.

3. Is there a place close to our residence where our dog can relieve himself without causing problems?

4. Are we willing to bear the costs connected with

Proper housing, scheduled feedings and regular socialization are just some of the things to consider before you acquire a Rottweiler.

owning a dog?

5. Can the dog come along when we leave for vacations or is there a boarding kennel where we can leave him without having to worry? If we have a kennel in mind we should make reservations early since such establishments fill up quickly during the vacation months.

6. Are we aware that we will no longer be welcome guests with certain relatives or friends as soon as we show up with a dog?

It is the costs that are frequently overlooked. People consider the purchase price but neglect the costs of feeding and caring for the dog, which should also include veterinary care. Per year, these costs usually exceed the purchase price by far. The veterinary care alone may cost that much if the dog should get sick or be involved in an accident.

Experience shows that such considerations hardly deter anyone from purchasing a dog. Nevertheless, it is important to ask oneself these questions. In that way, we are aware of our responsibilities from the outset. It is very hard to part, for whatever reason, with a dog one has come to love. It can be the consequence of a thoughtless purchase or the sad result of a lack of knowledge. Despite our best efforts, we learn that we cannot deal with the dog. This happens occasionally, especially with the Rottweiler who generally is of strong character. Sometimes, it is exactly the good qualities of a dog that bring about its failure as a pet and, in the end, it is usually the dog who suffers the most.

CHOOSING A BREEDER

It is important to see to what extent the environment of the kennel that we are considering to buy our Rottweiler from affects the development of a puppy's temperament in a positive or negative way. We should visit the kennel a few times when the puppies are four to ten weeks old. Even better, visit two or three different breeding establishments to compare. The effort will pay off because in doing so we will learn more than we ever could from a book. We will see

Use your judgment when selecting a Rottweiler pup and pick the one you like best. Better yet, pick the one who forthrightly picks you!

differences, and also get a
feeling as to which breeder's
way of raising dogs we like.
The addresses of the breeders
we can get from breed clubs.
The people there will also be
able to tell us where puppies
are available.

A breeder, sure of his work,
will be glad to see us even if
we make the appointment to
inspect the litter expressly

*Rottweiler puppies should
not be handled by strangers
until they have received their
first series of vaccinations.*

without obligation to make a purchase. He welcomes
the excitement visitors bring to his breeding
establishment since he knows that his puppies will
profit from a visit by strangers.

A good breeder will, of course, have an eye on order
and cleanliness in the kennel. Kennel and exercise areas
should provide the puppies with a variety of stimulating
objects with which to entertain themselves. The only
requirement: they should be safe so that the puppies
won't hurt themselves. The most important thing,
however, is that the ground offers the puppies a variety
of surfaces. This makes housebreaking much easier later
on. I have already mentioned how much this influences
the time required to housebreak the puppies. In a
kennel that is conducive for the puppies' development,
there will hardly ever be complete order, rather it will
present the impression of creative disorder.

If a kennel is located in idyllic isolation and quiet, we
should inquire if the breeder provides enough artificial
environmental stimulation for his puppies.

Caution is also advised whenever we come across a
breeding establishment where the set-up is overly
sterile, but we gain the impression that the set-up is
basically designed to save the breeder as much work
with the puppies as possible. Here we should refrain
from buying. Even the most talented puppy will not be

able to develop sufficiently under such conditions to be prepared for living with a new owner. By the way, we should be aware that this will not necessarily become noticeable immediately after the purchase, rather it will become evident only after the young dog has matured (i.e., at age nine to 12 months). Suddenly there may be shyness toward people and fearfulness when surrounded by traffic noise.

When we find a situation that we think is favorable for the raising of puppies, talk to the breeder. He can tell us about the parents and the behavior of the individual puppies. His observations are much more important than what is written in the pedigree. There we will see the names of champion ancestors. Even the best parents don't always produce conformation champions, and only dogs with which people have worked intensively obtain performance titles. There are also several instances of falsified or completely meaningless pedigrees. Thus, we should make certain that the pedigree presented to us has been issued by a national breed club.

A breeder will be able to tell you about the individual personalities of each puppy in a litter.

If you are planning on showing your Rottweiler in any type on competition be sure to look for championships in the pup's ancestry.

If we like the chosen breeder because he provides information freely and is pleased with our interest and inquiries, then we are at the right place. We can count on this breeder to provide helpful counsel in the future if we should encounter problems. This, for instance, could be the case if pathological changes not yet evident in the puppy later develop. Unfortunately, there is no way to prevent such occurrences entirely. In this regard, buying a puppy will always be somewhat of a gamble.

Once we have decided on a breeder, all that remains is choosing the puppy. Here the good breeder can be our best advisor. He has observed his litter daily and has

At five to seven weeks of age puppies start to enjoy actively socializing with their littermates and with humans.

noticed how differently the individual puppies behave. Of course, we too, will watch closely during our visit and see differences between the puppies. Some will be more active than others, some will seem to dominate their littermates, others less so. But we may be mistaken in what we believe we see on our visits. For instance, if a puppy should lie by himself away from the others the entire time without showing much energy, it could nevertheless be an otherwise active puppy that just happens to be, at the time of our visit, suffering from a bit of gas or feeling a bit under the weather. If we tell the breeder about our observations, we will find out whether or not he has made generally the same observation in regard to the puppy's behavior. Thus, talking to the breeder can save us from drawing the wrong conclusions.

But now, what are the criteria we want to apply for choosing a puppy? Certainly, we will like an alert and active animal that obviously displays social behavior toward its littermates. In the individual puppies of a litter there are differences in intensity as well as different degrees of dominance. If we want our Rottweiler to be a family dog and have no intentions of formal training, then we should not choose the most active and most dominant puppy. This would be a dog for a person more involved in dog sports or working dogs. Especially with Rottweilers, a dog that is noticeably calm as a puppy will be everything that we can wish a family dog to be.

A puppy's needs at an early age are simple: warmth, food and lots of sleep.

We can now see that we should choose our puppy with an eye to the purpose for which we want to acquire him, and a good breeder, thanks to his experience, will be able to provide excellent counsel.

Not recommended, in general, are puppies that always keep to themselves away from the rest of the litter and fearfully retreat from us whenever we approach them or those puppies that clearly impress us as nervous.

Now, it does happen that a potential owner, on his very first visit, spontaneously decides on one particular puppy that, by chance, is the first to approach him or gets noticed for some other reason—an imploring look from dark eyes, distinct coloration of the coat, some appealing form of behavior. But before he makes the decision to buy, he should first consult the breeder. Frequently it is no longer possible to dissuade the buyer from his choice. Still, disappointment is not inevitable. Even if the prognosis was not good, many acquisitions that came about this way have turned out to be fortuitous.

The deliberations presented here only apply when there still is a choice. If only one puppy is available, we should scrutinize the little one especially carefully to determine whether he has faults that can already be detected at this early age or whether he is especially shy, lacking in social behavior or nervous.

Puppies need exposure to plenty of new locations and stimuli. The more positive human contact he can receive, the better.

As can be seen from all this, it is advantageous to visit and observe the growing litter a number of times as long as there is the opportunity to make a choice. As early as three weeks of age we can observe different levels of activity among the puppies. Beginning with the sixth week, we should, now and then, take one of the puppies in which we are interested out of the litter and let him come to know us, perhaps on the lawn, and play with him, always being careful not to stress him. A breeder who is interested in his puppies will gladly accompany us. Away from their accustomed surroundings, the puppies always behave somewhat differently, less secure without the company of their littermates. It will thus be easier to

Once Rottweilers mature from puppyhood, they generally prefer the attention of humans to the companionship of another dog.

puppy has begun to become more independent and to turn away from the mother. Thus, this is quite a favorable time for the puppy to leave, but on the other hand the puppy has not yet had very much opportunity to practice his social skills with his littermates. Thus, he is not yet as secure in interactions with other dogs as he needs to be for future encounters.

If we, despite this, take him in at age eight weeks we should continually bring him together with other dogs and not, out of simple fear, keep him away from them. A Rottweiler puppy is extremely sturdy and can take quite a bit. He should experience as many encounters as possible and be allowed to romp with other young dogs. If, however, we were to buy our Rottweiler from a place that provides little variety for the puppies, then taking him at age eight weeks can only be advantageous, because this is the time when he is especially able to accept and assimilate experiences.

A puppy can be taken home without any worries at age ten weeks or even 12 weeks. This has the advantage that the first three sets of

A Rottweiler puppy can safely be taken home at ten to twelve weeks of age.

inoculations should have been given. Additionally, in this way, the puppies will spend a good part of the socialization phase in their pack, which, in every respect, can only be to the good for their development.

However, at age 16 weeks or older there is the danger of a temperament loss. This can be the result of a lack of contact with people as well as of being intimidated by older animals. With puppies of this age, we must expect that their adaptation to their new home will require considerably more effort and probably will never be as optimal as it could have been at an earlier point in time. Unless the seller, during this period, took the young dog into his house and treated him as his own animal.

PICKING UP THE PUPPY

For a reputable seller there is no question that he will point out to the potential owner any shortcomings in the puppy that may have become apparent by this time (i.e., if a male should have only one testicle or none, which will disqualify him from breeding and conformation). He

Although all puppies are irresistible, purchase your Rottweiler puppy when you find the one that you feel will be best for you.

will provide information about the health and temperament status of the parents. When the parents have been x-rayed for hip dysplasia, a hereditary deformation of the hip joint, he will show us the findings. In most instances, the pedigree will not yet be available when we pick up the puppy, but you should receive the registration papers that will show that our puppy is really a purebred whom we will later be able to enter in shows and participate in dog sports. Normally, the seller will also give us the puppy's health record into which he will have entered the first inoculations against distemper, infectious hepatitis, leptospirosis, parvo, and frequently kennel cough and

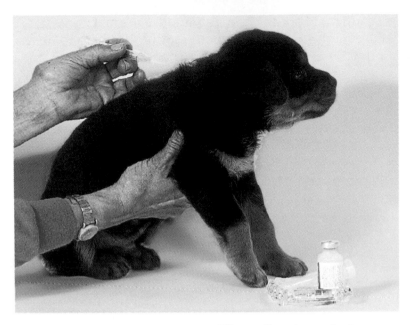

The puppy's first set of inoculations should be given at six to eight weeks of age, the second set at ten to 12 weeks, and the third at 14 to 16 weeks.

corona. These first inoculations provide some immunity but must be repeated a few weeks later. Under no circumstances should we forget to do so.

It is good to know what, how often, and how much the puppy was given to eat during the last week and what kind of food the seller recommends we use. It would be best to continue feeding the food the breeder used, in regard to both quality and quantity. A change of food at this point, when the puppy is already somewhat stressed psychologically, should be avoided. For that reason, many sellers will send some food along as well as a brief feeding plan.

Before we take our puppy home, we should once more go carefully over him. He should be as alert as always, with a shiny coat without any sore spots that might be eczematous; clean ears; and clear eyes without any discharge. The gums and mouth should not show any inflamed spots. Stools should be normal and the anal region should show no traces of diarrhea. In males, both testicles should be clearly present. A reputable seller will explain and demonstrate all this on his own. But it may happen that something is forgotten so it is good for owners to also have this information beforehand.

Nowadays it has become customary to sign a sales contract in which the seller certifies that he knows of no apparent or hidden faults or diseases in the animal in question. The potential owner acknowledges that he has inspected the dog. He also agrees not to bring any claims in regard to acquired or inherited defects that might become apparent later, that pertain to conformation, temperament, or health of the dog and, as far as is humanly possible, could not be seen or predicted at the time of sale.

When it comes time for you to take your new puppy home, try to bring him home early in the day so that he has an opportunity to explore his new environment before bedtime.

When the moment has arrived when we put the puppy under our arm, so to speak, in order to take him joyfully home, then we must once more think about how everything is supposed to progress from here on. That can only be done if we have discussed, days earlier, with the family, how we will proceed when our little Rottweiler moves into our home as the new quadruped member of the family.

PURCHASING AN ADULT ROTTWEILER

If we buy a puppy from a reputable establishment who takes care to raise puppies in a way that furthers their development, then chances are good that we acquire a Rottweiler that later will be a pleasure to own. Certainly, after the dog comes to us we will have to properly care for him and train him, and that will, especially in the first few months, require quite a bit of time. But this effort also brings a lot of joy. Since dogs can remain adaptable until old age, it is quite possible to have good luck when purchasing an adult dog. But it is just as likely that we buy trouble if we do not clarify a number of things ahead of time.

If you are acquiring an older dog, be sure to investigate whether or not it has been exposed to children.

First, we should find out why the dog is being given away. That's not always easy. In a pound, people will only be able to pass on to us what the former owner/ finder told them. It is rather obvious that these statements frequently have nothing in common with reality because no one likes to admit that as a dog owner he was a failure. The owner himself will provide only evasive answers. Thus, whenever no credible information is available, caution is called for. Especially, since in the beginning, the dog will normally be on his best behavior in his new surroundings until, as he grows more and more at home, his confidence grows. Only now will he reveal those bad traits that may have been the reason why the former owner gave him away. And that can go on, step by step, for up to six months before we know for sure what kind of dog we bought. Of course, we can try to retrain him whenever he suddenly displays a new form of misbehavior. However, such retraining may easily require more effort than raising a puppy into a well-brought-up young dog would have. Furthermore, we can only expect to be successful in this if we possess enough knowledge to proceed in a clear and consistent manner.

Ultimate submission for a dog is to lie on its back and expose its belly.

Second, if at all possible, we should find out where and under what conditions the dog in question spent his days as a puppy. If we should learn that he spent the first ten to 12 weeks of his life in a propitious environment, we may expect that, in time, he will become well acclimated to his new home and will behave well. It will also be possible to reduce or overcome fearfulness. Thus, it would be the ideal thing if we could contact the dog's original breeder, visit him, and ask questions. Maybe all our reservations will resolve.

Circumstances for a successful adoption of an older dog are always favorable if we are familiar with the conditions of his former home from our own observations. In that case, the former owners are not unknown to us and we can have a frank discussion about why they want to part with their dog.

If the first owner can advance a credible explanation and if he reports frankly about the dog's behavior up to this point, then we may be reassured and gladly offer the dog a new home without taking any major risk.

However, whatever the situation, the first thing to do is to take the dog away from his accustomed surroundings for a few hours or even days, take a walk with him, take him home with us. Thus we will learn if the dog shows normal sociability or if he becomes more restless, fearful and withdrawn further away from his familiar territory. One should never omit this test.

The recommendations that will be made on to how to train puppies and young dogs can also be applied to any adult or elderly dog. Of course, we must expect to have to make a somewhat greater effort. But by proceeding purposefully, deliberately and calmly we will be, sooner or later, successful. The experimental division of the Swiss Society for Rescue Dogs repeatedly trained older dogs in order to demonstrate the dogs' ability to learn. An eight-year-old Boxer who, at first, was totally unresponsive after a few exercises became more and more eager to work and, as a result, also more capable of learning. After one year, he was ready to take the Schutzhund I test.

Training your Rottweiler must be approached in a deliberate, purposeful and calm manner.

PUPPY CARE and Training

W here is our dog to sleep and eat?
Which rooms is he not to enter?
Where is he allowed to relieve himself?
Who will feed him?

Where is the dog to spend the first night?

What will we do from the beginning to facilitate housebreaking and who shall be responsible for it?

One of the first items you need for the new Rottweiler puppy is a Nylabone for his growing teeth. Be sure to buy the right size.

All these questions should have been raised and answered among the family before we set out to bring the puppy home. If this isn't done, we will be overwhelmed once the youngster is home and begins to investigate everything. He will make his first puddle on the best carpet in the house and the result of that will be excited discussions and differences of opinions among the family members. This can be prevented by discussing the questions listed above before we, full of expectations, arrive at the breeder's door where that little Rottweiler who will spend his next ten years or more with our family is waiting for us.

THE TRIP HOME

Our puppy is still extremely receptive and adaptable, but also correspondingly sensitive. And now, more than later, all events that he experiences for the first time will leave a deep impression on him. For this reason we must act with caution. The following sequence of events, unfortunately occurring all too often, may illustrate this better than my warning words.

On pick-up day, the new owner places the puppy in the back seat (or possibly even in the passenger seat) of

the car and drives off. Sometime during the trip the puppy begins to vomit, but the owner expected that and took precautions with a plastic sheet. So, let's keep moving as fast as possible. Once at home the puppy will soon recover. After a few minutes with firm ground under his feet, the puppy begins to behave quite normally again. But, unfortunately, this rough procedure has left a deep impression. The next time we lift him into the car, he will become sick even before we start driving. And it will be this way with this dog for months, if not years. The owner's thoughtlessness has turned him into a notoriously carsick canine. Now we are really in a fix. It will be much better if we adhere to the following rules:

1. During the trip, a person takes care of the puppy, holds him, distracts him, plays with him (preferably using an object that carries the smell of the place he just left such as a rag).

2. After a few minutes of driving we stop at a suitable location and walk the puppy, on or off leash, for some time. Additionally, we offer him some water (bring a bowl).

3. When resuming the trip, we keep the puppy under constant observation and at the first sign of carsickness

When transporting your puppy home, be sure to stop several times on the side of the road to give the pup a break.

(heavy drooling, excessive panting, restlessness), we stop again and proceed as described above.

4. If the puppy remains calm when we resume the trip, and even begins to doze, then we can complete our journey without any further stops, taking care to reduce speed on winding roads.

During the car ride home one person should take care of the puppy in order to make his trip home as comfortable as possible.

If the puppy is shipped to us in a shipping crate either by railroad or airline—an acceptable way of transport—we will walk him for half an hour and offer him water (repeatedly in small amounts) before we continue his journey in our car. By the way, it is astonishing how well puppies and adult dogs manage railroad or airplane trips. The crates remain for long periods in relatively quiet locations so that the animals apparently get used to their environment. Frequently, they will be wide awake and happy shortly after leaving their crates.

Arrival at Home

Before we take the puppy into the house, we carry him directly from the car to that place in the yard or close to the house that we have selected as the main location for him to do his business. There we allow him to move around, on or off leash and without efforts at controlling him, until he urinates on his own. And we say to him, with an encouraging and praising voice, the first verbal command that he is to learn: "Go potty" or something similar. Thus the dog will make a connection between the pleasant sensation of elimination and our mildly spoken command. Soon we will be able to induce the dog to urinate and later also to defecate by means of this command, which never should be given as an urgent order but rather always in a patient coaxing way. And thus, with little effort, we have accomplished a lot. We could observe in this example how the dog made an association. Beginning with this important moment, whatever we will demand from our dog in the way of behavior in the future he will learn the fastest, the most certain, and the most lasting by creating such connections.

Not until after this first act of eliminating in home territory do we bring the dog into the house and into our living quarters.

INSIDE BEHAVIOR

Not all breeders make the effort to accustom their puppies to various inside rooms. Thus it may happen that our Rottweiler needs some time to find his way around and feel at ease. Preferably, we will carry him into the house so that a dark entrance hall with a slippery floor and a flight of steps will not make him feel insecure. Those who do not intend to allow the dog inside the house may take him immediately to the kennel, an environment that presumably will seem familiar to him and distress him less. However, Rottweilers are fundamentally unsuited to live exclusively in kennels. If we want to establish a good relationship with him, then the Rottweiler belongs inside the house, at least at first.

We should allow the puppy time to investigate the

These two Rottie pups are looking at a grasshopper for the first time.

Your Rottweiler puppy should be taken outside at regular scheduled intervals to eliminate.

room into which we brought him. Do not allow children to descend upon him right away and treat him like a toy. We should wait for the puppy to ask for attention and human contact by himself. Right now he has a lot to do. After all, he must process a large amount of unfamiliar scents and new visual impressions. For this reason, he will be very busy sniffing everything. Watching him do that is so interesting that we easily forget the time. That's why we should set the kitchen timer for 30 minutes and then carry the dog outside again to where he is to eliminate. It will be to our advantage if we do this every half hour until we retire to bed—on this day preferably as late as possible. Since we will have done all kinds of things with the youngster, he will be quite tired.

First thing in the morning, we carry him outside again. Proceeding in this way, we learn to observe the puppy's behavior in regard to elimination. Soon we will be able to recognize with a fair degree of certainty when the time has come. At the same time, the dog will learn that we take his eliminating seriously and will praise him for it at that certain place outside. Soon we will be able to extend the waiting periods, but we will always take him outside shortly before and after every meal.

We offer the puppy his very first meal after he has calmed down a bit. Of course, this, too, takes place at a location decided on ahead of time.

The First Night

In the beginning, we may be less consistent as to the place where the puppy will sleep. We have prepared a sleeping place in the center of our living quarters in the form of a shallow box or basket with a soft surface to lie on. During the first day, we have put the puppy in it with a toy, which still carries the scent of his former kennel. But to leave the puppy alone in the hallway and to close all doors when everyone goes to bed simply is asking too much of him. Up to this day, he has always had the warmth of his littermates and has never had to sleep alone. And then there is the strange room with its unfamiliar smells and noises. And so the little guy finds himself helpless and all alone. Those who think that they have to enforce their will from the very beginning without yielding an inch do not have any understanding of a dog's personality. They will remain unaware of how ineffectively they act, even after the puppy's incessant whining and howling have forced them to give in. Now

While it is necessary for a new puppy to play with and be loved by his new family, a young puppy tires easily and needs many naps each day.

the puppy has gotten his way and he will mark it down. As experience has shown, the juvenile dog, sooner or later, will start using the bed assigned to him on his own volition, even if we allow him to spend the first few nights with our bedroom door open. In most cases, he will lie down next to our bed and we can reach down to him with our hand to reassure him.

Your Rottweiler will find his own special place where he can go for some rest and relaxation.

In the early morning hours, it would not be a rare occurrence that the youngster begins to whine because he wants to go outside. Immediately we should pick him up and carry him to the outside. This likely will lead to our first success in the housebreaking effort.

This does not mean that he is fully housebroken, there will be setbacks—especially if we are not vigilant enough. But the path has been opened and success will not remain elusive. Dogs that were well prepared by the breeder and are treated sensibly at their new home will be housebroken in a few days. If there should be an accident inside, we must keep our cool, immediately carry the dog to his accustomed place, even if the need has been taken care of already. If we were to scold our dog, we would confuse him to such a degree that the misbehavior is reinforced. If he now begins to eliminate almost exclusively inside, then that has nothing to do with stubbornness, but rather it is the result of our actions that frightened and totally confused the youngster. There are still dog books that recommend rubbing the dog's nose into the stool that was deposited in the wrong place as an effective training tool. This is not true. It is always wrong to attempt to force a dog to do something, before we are sure that he has had the opportunity to understand what it is that we want him to do.

What I have said about how we should treat the newly arrived puppy applies for the first two or three days in his new home.

THE FIRST TWO WEEKS

During this period it is important that we devote enough time to our Rottweiler so that he can become properly acclimated. We should not overtax him or allow him too many liberties. That, however, does not mean that we cannot show him where he fits in and get him used to the collar and leash, if this was not done so already.

We can let him know what he is not to do under any circumstances by establishing taboos. For instance, we may keep him away, with a gentle but forceful shove, from those rooms that he is not to enter. Normally, he will soon respond to such corrections by respecting these boundaries. However, if he finds this difficult to do, we should welcome it because it indicates a certain intensity and insistence that will be of great use to us and him in the future. Nevertheless, we shall, persistently and patiently, continue with our corrections until success has been achieved.

On or near his bed, we deposit some suitable chew devices such as Nylabone® or Gumabone® products made especially for puppies. And in those times when the youngster excitedly seeks contact with us and grabs our hands, arms, and feet with his sharp little milk teeth, we will play with him, fetch his toys and entertain him

with them. To reject the youngster in this state of internal excitement and readiness for contact, just because we are sitting in

Whether your Rottweiler is a puppy or an adult it will enjoy playing with its Nylabone® products.

Punishing your Rottweiler puppy is meaningless unless you catch him in the act. Ideally, catch him before he begins something undesirable and redirect his attentions.

front of the TV, is both uncivilized and harmful to the dog. If we don't participate in his games he will entertain himself and, in all likelihood, cause some damage. Once it has happened, punishment is meaningless since the dog is not able to make the connection between this punishment and an event that has already passed. But we will keep an eye on him and intervene whenever he gets ready to chew on the carpet or a chair leg. Preferably, we will throw something that is in easy reach and cannot hurt him close to where he is about to do something undesirable. At the same time we may say, "No" in a calm voice, and soon we will be able with this "No" to slow him down and keep him from doing something that is forbidden, whenever he is about to do just that.

CONTACTS WITH OTHER DOGS

Especially in the beginning we should take our Rottweiler, as often as possible, to meet other dogs. He is extremely sturdy and it won't hurt him if, in play, he should end up under an older dog. Harm will be done, however, if we continually keep him away, with excited words or pulling on the leash, from playing freely with other dogs or even from establishing contact with them. By giving him no opportunity to come to terms with other dogs on his own, we make him timid. He needs such experiences in order to become independent and confident. Then, there won't be any difficulties with other dogs once he is an adult. Even if he should attempt later to dominate (i.e., shoving and trying to mount an animal of the same sex), his aggression will be limited. He will grab but not injure the other dog through biting. That is important for our powerful and spirited Rottweiler. We should begin to pay attention to these matters when our Rottweiler is still a juvenile.

GRABBING WITH THE MOUTH

Since the milk teeth are pointed and sharp, there may very well be some scratches whenever our dog grabs us with his mouth. His bite inhibition is set to the skin thickness of his littermates, and we have a considerably thinner skin. However, if we were to roughly reject the dog whenever he makes a grab for us, this would only frustrate him. We must keep in mind that dogs use their mouth to touch and investigate everything. They don't have any hands to feel with, caress with, grab with, and carry with. It is their mouth

Rather than pushing your pup away when being mouthed, let out a loud yelp and your pup should cease to grab so hard.

Leash training is one of the most important things you can teach your Rottweiler.

with which they express all their friendliness and love. It would be difficult for our dog if we were to continually push him away, more or less violently, because we fear that this might be the beginning of a biting problem. A loud cry of pain, on the other hand, may keep him from grabbing all too hard just as it did with his littermates. That he can "understand," and he will grab with less force. This very process is an act of early communication between owner and his dog.

GOING FOR WALKS AND LEAD TRAINING

If, in the beginning, the young Rottweiler refuses to walk on a leash with us, coaxing or yelling won't help as long as the leash is held taut. The best thing to do is to use the leash to pull the dog close and then immediately relax all tension on the leash. Now we are in a position to encourage the youngster, with words or treats, to walk on. After we have repeated this process a number of times, the dog will relax and begin to walk with us. Soon he will forge ahead, especially if we are on ground with

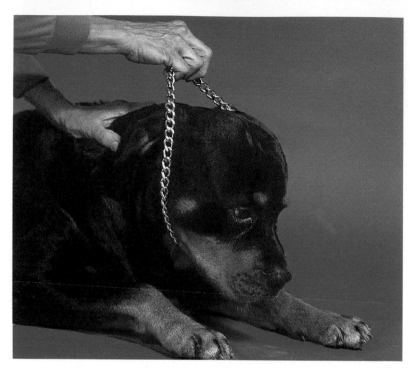

It is advisable not to use a chain collar when first teaching your Rottweiler to walk on a leash. This type of collar will be useful later on.

which he is already familiar. We should not attempt to break him from this forging on a tight leash at this time. He still weighs so little that keeping him under control is no problem. It is advisable, however, not to use a collar that is too thin or a chain collar. A wide leather collar is best. It is easy on the throat area of the dog. Chain collars will be useful in the future, but when dogs are playing with other dogs, we should take them off. There is the danger that dogs, in playful fights, will bite on them and lose their canine teeth. Thus we will also watch out that our Rottweiler's playmates are not wearing chain collars.

At first, we will not go on extended hikes with our Rottweiler, but we will certainly take him on regular walks. It is important for his recall behavior in the future that, on these walks, we keep moving without calling the dog continuously. If his "pack" is continually moving away from him, the young dog will grow accustomed to pay attention to its location. He will follow on his own accord and we can call him when he is already coming. Thus he will soon grasp the meaning of our command. Whenever the dog is distracted to such an extent that he no longer follows, it would be very wrong to repeatedly call him to come. The proper procedure is that we do not ask too much of our dog and simply go and get him. This

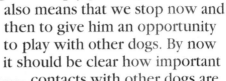

It is important that you allow your Rottweiler to come into contact with many different situations while out for a walk.

also means that we stop now and then to give him an opportunity to play with other dogs. By now it should be clear how important

contacts with other dogs are for our young Rottweiler. But it is just as important that he comes into contact with as many and as different people as possible, including children. We need not fear that our Rottweiler might develop into a dog that wants to be friends with all the world. We can put our absolute trust in his pronounced feeling of belonging, provided, of course, that we offer him whatever he needs to feel secure, active, and well content.

Unfortunately, there are many dog owners who take their dog for a walk without much thought or attention to him. They prefer to give way to their own thoughts or to talk endlessly with other dog owners also out for a walk. The result is that the dog no longer experiences the world together with his owner. No deepened relationship comes about between the dog and his owner. And yet every walk with the young dog provides the very best opportunity for building mutual understanding and trust.

FEEDING the Rottweiler

A new puppy should be fed according to the feeding regimen he has been accustomed to. The dog himself usually lets us know that feeding twice a day is sufficient. This may happen soon or somewhat later; each dog has his own peculiarities. It would not be wrong if we were to feed the adult dog twice a day. That would reduce the stress on his stomach and can also be a precaution against canine bloat, which unfortunately, does occur in all midsize and large dog breeds, including the Rottweiler. Normally, however, people will, at some time, start feeding only once a day. It is the rule in training courses for working and service dogs.

What we feed, at first, is determined by the seller's recommendation. If the dog does well on that food, is alert and healthy, then there is no reason to change. Dogs are not set on variety, and most commercial foods contain everything dogs need. Kibble with small pieces of meat containing large doses of preservatives that are sold as "balanced diets" should not be fed exclusively. These preservatives put a heavy strain on the metabolism. It is better to feed the dog a meatless kibble adding fresh

Feed your Rottweiler puppy what it has been accustomed to eating. If you must change his diet, do so gradually to avoid a stomach upset.

meat one day (no uncooked pork—danger of trichinosis and the fatal Aujeszky's disease or pseudorabies) and canned meat the next. Thus, the dog gets used to both and we won't have any digestive problems with him when we go on vacation and may have only one or the other available. Kibble should be soaked, the liquid will be gone in about ten minutes and the food is ready to be served. Additionally, the dog should always have access to fresh water in a separate container. If the dog should develop an itch as a reaction to a particular kibble mix and scratch noticeably often, we should change the type of kibble we use. Not all dogs tolerate all mixes equally well.

Mother's milk supplied your puppy with all of his basic food needs as well as with a natural ability to fight off many diseases.

Your Rottweiler puppy should be permitted to eat comfortably and privately with no distractions. His crate is the best place for this.

Dog food manufacturers include into their products all the vitamins and minerals that a dog needs. This makes further additives unnecessary. The only question is whether or not our dog

absorbs the additives in the form that they are provided. Another as of yet unanswered question is whether or not the fresh meat that is the natural main food of the dog contains substances that cannot be added to commercial foods. This alone is reason enough for me to recommend adding fresh meat to the diet whenever the opportunity presents itself.

There is no formula to determine how much food a dog should eat, not even when we know his body weight. Each dog is unique and the differences can be quite large. One may get along fine with small amounts of food, another may need a lot more. Thus, we let the dog's nutritional state be our measuring stick; a state that, in the case of the Rottweiler, can easily be recognized with the naked eye. A glossy coat and a musculature that, at least when in motion, visibly stands out, are the signs of good nutrition. General liveliness and noticeable well-

It is important for your Rottweiler's elimination behavior that he be fed on a regular schedule.

being are such signs as well. Thinness, however, that shows the bones, is an alarming sign of malnutrition or illness and, in most cases, the coat will be dull as well.

Fresh clean water is essential to your Rottweiler's well being.

Whether or not the food agrees with our dog can be seen by his stool. Normally the stool deposited first is somewhat firmer than the stool deposited somewhat later. If the latter should appear a bit too soft or even runny then that is not yet a cause for worry. However, we should observe the dog when he has his next stool.

It is important for the dog's elimination behavior that we feed as much as possible at the same time every day. Then he will adjust his defecating as it fits best, for him and us, into our daily routines. Dogs that are fed at regular times and are taken for walks at equally regular times, will, as a rule, retain their stool until this walk, since they can tolerate deviations of one or two hours without much trouble. This, apparently, has to do with their inner need to use their stool for marking.

TIPS FOR FEEDING

1. Young dogs should be fed two to three times daily, and adult dogs two times daily.

2. Whatever age your dog is, he should always be fed at the same time. The dog will adjust to his meal time and will patiently wait until then. He will not beg.

3. Always feed your dog in the same place and from the same (clean) bowl. The eating place should be protected against sun, rain, and wind, and be located in a quiet undisturbed area.

Your dog should always have access to water, especially in hot weather and when outdoors.

4. Feed your dog a food on which he does well. Food should not be too cold nor too hot, but rather lukewarm.

5. Fit the amount of food to the need of the dog. Additional treats should be given regularly, not at the whim of dog or master.

6. Never feed at the dinner table!

7. The dog should always have access to water in a separate bowl.

Caution! Do not feed before walks or sporting events.

Be sure to fit the amount of food to the need of the dog. Puppies require several smaller meals in a day, but not all adults require the same amount.

EVERYDAY CARE for Your Rottweiler

The Rottweiler needs plentiful, regular, and occasionally extensive exercise. Of course, we will not overtax the very young dog, but there is also no reason to be overly protective of him. By nature, he is an animal that needs to be active and we should take this into account.

Basically, a dog does not need much space to sleep and eat, but he urgently needs exercise and something to do. He finds exercise on walks and hikes and when playing with other dogs. Here, he can develop his muscles and strengthen his tendons and joints. It is a widely held error that a dog will exercise himself if he has a large yard available. He will keep busy in his own way. If he feels neglected, he will dig up flower beds, race along the fence and bark at and pursue passers-by, or come up with other activities that surely will not please us.

With the young dog, we should take two short walks and one longer one every day. On these he should meet as many other dogs as possible and be allowed to sniff them. To walk him less than an hour a day simply is not enough.

Your Rottweiler will get a great deal of exercise from walking, hiking and playing with other dogs.

Beyond exercise, the Rottweiler needs little care. We will brush him now and then, but not with a hard brush because his skin under his coat is sensitive. Brushing, even with a plastic or rubber curry comb, can produce small abrasions that may turn into areas of inflammation. When the Rottweiler is in the shedding period, the short hairs can best be removed with a damp sponge or buckskin, both from the dog and from furniture and carpets.

It is also part of caring for our Rottweiler that we observe him every day in order to be able to recognize irregularities in his constitution or his behavior. Those who really interact with their dogs, even as little as half an hour twice a day, will not miss changes in behavior.

If our Rottweiler attains the age of eight years without suffering from any ailment, we can be content. If he is still in great shape when reaching ten years, we can consider ourselves fortunate. Anything beyond ten years is a gift from the fates and is quite within the realm of the possible.

By observing your Rottweiler on a daily basis you will come to know irregularities in his constitution or behavior.

BASIC TRAINING for the Rottweiler

The first three or four months of a Rottweiler's life determine what kind of dog we will have at the end. Of course, the dog's inherited temperament plays an important role as well, but this we cannot change. What we—and before us the breeder—can do is to deliberately foster the dog's natural traits so that he will be adaptable and confident. If we make serious efforts to influence our Rottweiler in this way, he, now about four months old and a juvenile, will be optimally prepared for his future task, whether as family dog and companion, or as sport, utility or rescue dog. Without such expert preparation as a puppy, we would have to expect our dog to be difficult in all respects later on.

A well-trained Rottweiler is not only a pleasure to his owner, but to strangers as well.

An essential point during this period of preparation is the dog's trust in his human partner, a trust that was systematically built during this time. This will enable us in the future to communicate with him. In the process of communication we will, again and again, make mistakes, in most cases because we misjudge his ability to comprehend. A well-prepared dog, however, will not be thrown by that. His basic trust in us enables him to overcome uncertainties and misunderstandings whenever they

Your Rottweiler will learn to trust you from early puppy training. This trust will enable you to communicate with him in the future.

arise, and to remain responsive to corrections.

It would be a pity if we were to discontinue working with and training our dog once the preparation phase is over. It is not that we can afford to wait until he will, so to speak, "enter school" later. On the contrary, what we can successfully teach him now will make it unnecessary for him to attend a so-called training course later. Participants in such a course practice things that a sensibly brought up dog has learned a long time ago and is accustomed to apply in everyday life.

What I am going to recommend here does not take a lot of time but does require some self-discipline and concentration. It is very much worthwhile doing. We will build the exercises into those routine daily events such as leaving the house, passing the front gate, crossing the street, entering and getting out of the car. And further, being off-leash on walks and being called in order to be leashed.

SETTING OUT FOR A WALK

It is best to use a leather leash with two snap hooks: one hook allows us to shorten the leash to one-half of its length and the other snaps into the ring on the collar. If our dog is a "leash killer" we may use a light chain when we want to tie him up, but we should never walk the dog on such a chain. That could be dangerous for our hands. It is not infrequent that tendons are partly cut or severed when a dog jerks forcefully on the chain and the chain's

links wrap themselves around a finger. A simple, not too narrow leather band makes an excellent collar. A chain collar, by itself, is

Teaching your Rottweiler to "heel" will make outings more enjoyable for both of you.

useful, but it could happen that other dogs may damage one of their teeth on it when playing with our dog. Whenever we want to go out with our dog, we first show him the collar and put it on him while talking encouragingly or we let him slip into

It is not good to forcibly walk your puppy on a leash. First, show him his collar and then put it on him while talking encouragingly or let him slip into it.

it, something he will soon do gladly since it means going out. If we do not have a front yard, we will put him on the leash before going through the front door. The ritual of putting on a leash goes like this:

1. Firmly but gently, we pull the dog to our left side, grip his collar with our right hand and lift him up a bit and help him—with the fingertips of our left hand tapping on his croup—to assume a sitting position.

2. Only after he has done so and is sitting properly, do we slowly lower the collar again while saying in a

friendly voice "Sit."

3. Now we stand upright and wait a second or two. If the dog gets up we say in a friendly and calm voice (not in a peremptory tone!) "No" and, without any further words, put him back into a sitting position as described above.

4. Now we put on the leash which we have been carrying over our shoulders or in a pocket to keep it out of the way.

For the time being, we do not yet correct the young dog if he should get up and attempt to push out the door while we are attaching the leash. In the course of a few weeks, however, we will expect him to remain sitting until we tell him with the command "heel" to walk with us. By that time, however, our dog should sit almost on his own accord at front door and yard gate.

A collar and leash are vital tools for training your Rottweiler.

We will proceed in this way when coming to the curb of the sidewalk before crossing a street: First make him sit, then praise him briefly and, after a short pause, ask him to come along. Here, too, we will demand in time that the dog reliably remain sitting until we give him the command to continue walking. Whenever we cross a street we should once more make the dog sit when we reach the other side, without changing direction (i.e., with our backs to the street). Thus the dog will soon realize that we are always heading for a spot where he will have to sit once again. Later, when we cross a street with him off-leash, he won't run off immediately but will remain under our control until we reach the opposite sidewalk.

Teaching your Rottweiler to sit is one of the basic commands in obedience training.

We will proceed exactly the same way before getting into our car and will do the same thing to our advantage whenever we

The most basic commands you could ever teach your Rottweiler are SIT, HEEL, DOWN, COME *and* STAY.

come to the first step of a flight of stairs that we want to go up or down. Let us not forget that our Rottweiler not only is powerful and lively but will also gain in weight. We must accustom him now, while we are still strong enough to enforce it, to allow himself to be controlled by us. Teaching such complacent behavior to an adult Rottweiler could turn into heavy labor that only a specialist might be able to perform.

Through this process of making him sit, we attract his attention, and the necessary basic mood, whenever we must let him know that he has to stay by our side and heed our commands. If we are consistent, this will become second nature to our young dog. And it all happens without fuss and we will not have to roar commands that the dog does not understand.

THE STAY EXERCISE

This exercise not only serves as training for the dog but also provides the dog owner with the knowledge he will need in order to communicate with his dog. If we give the dog a chance to realize what we want him to do, he will, out of his innate need to please, gladly do it. He is not an opponent whom we have to force to obey but our partner with different, but nevertheless considerable, talents of his own, who is more than willing to adapt to us. He can learn easily if we act in such a way that does not overtax his ability to comprehend. The stay exercise is easy to carry through for both us and the dog and is a good way to observe the process of learning as the dog masters it. After a certain amount of focused practice (at most once a day for five minutes, later a bit longer), we will become very confident as to how we interact with our dog. We will then know how we can influence him and he will become attentive to what we are doing and will grow accustomed to do our bidding.

Heeling is especially important along walks where strangers might be encountered. No one likes a strange dog that approaches them off lead.

Step by step, we proceed as follows:

1. Holding the end of the leash in our right hand and with our dog following on our left side, we march a straight line at a good pace. Then at some point we execute an about turn to the right and march in the opposite direction, without having said a word to the dog or making physical contact. The dog will soon adjust to our constant speed.

If he follows at our side well, we briefly pat him with our left hand and praise him, "Good dog. Heel." If he forges ahead on the leash, we repeat our about turn, without a word and as always to the right, so that the leash is in front of us and we pull the dog with our entire weight behind us.

2. After some back and forth, we grip the leash with our left hand just above the collar and, still walking ahead, lift the dog up a bit.

3. Now we slow down and finally stop, always keeping the dog slightly lifted by the collar. In this position, we pass the leash to our right hand in order to make the dog sit by tapping him with the fingertips of our left hand on the croup. If he does sit, we will, after a brief pause, relax the leash slowly until there is no longer any pull on the dog's neck and the leash is loose again. While we relax the tension on the leash, we say slowly and in a friendly voice, "Sit." After a moment, we pat the dog's head (with the left hand) and say, "Good dog. Sit."

Note: So far, this has been a heel and sit exercise, which should always precede the stay exercise.

4. Now we hold the palm of our left hand (fingers together) in front of the dog's head just as long as it takes to say, "Stay" (not peremptorily spoken but rather slowly and in a friendly voice). Then we withdraw our hand. Except for this hand signal, we have not moved at all—we did not bend forward nor did we turn toward the dog.

5. After pausing for about one second, we step in front

All initial training of your Rottweiler should be done on a leash. Not until your dog's education is complete and dependable should you leave him off lead.

of the dog, still holding the leash at its very end. We do not do this tentatively but rather with two or three quick steps.

If the dog remains sitting, we now reinforce his behavior from the front. We say, "Good dog. Stay," while at the same time holding our left palm in front of him and withdraw it again with the end of the verbal command.

Do not make training sessions too long. When your Rottweiler is responding favorably, reward him and end the session on a good note.

If the dog breaks the sit, this is no reason for us to be angry, but rather we are happy that he is giving us an opportunity to calmly say, "No." For this "No" is an important aid in the communication between owner and dog. It will soon become a signal for the dog that he has done something undesirable that will always bring a mild correction, that in time he will even expect. Later, we will use this "No" to slow the dog down and to attract his attention so that he will be more receptive for a successful correction. In the case of the stay exercise, the correction always is to make the dog sit at exactly the same spot as before, to do it in exactly the same way as before, and to restart the stay exercise from the very beginning.

6. It is quite possible that the dog will follow us for a number of times whenever we step in front of him after the "Stay." Perhaps, in rare cases, he will do this as often as ten times or more; or a dog may try to evade us or to block us. This dog does not yet know his proper place. We may be glad that this exercise—properly carried out— will give us the opportunity to remedy the situation. Prerequisites for success are that we act calmly and precisely. When the dog stays in the sit, either from the beginning or after a few repetitions, or when we step in front of him, and after we have said, together with the hand signal, our reinforcing "Good dog. Stay," we should remain standing in front of him for a while (varying the

length of time from exercise to exercise), relaxed and not looking at him.

7. Without any other movement we again show the dog our palm, accompanying this hand signal with the command "Stay," and immediately withdraw our hand.

8. After waiting for about one second, we briskly return to the dog where we will remain standing, upright and calmly, for an additional second. The waiting periods described here are important because they help fit the process to the dog's ability to comprehend. So that we do not forget the pauses, we will make it a habit to think or say something like "one Mississippi."

9. Now we praise the dog petting him with our left hand and saying, "Good dog. Stay." We must not be too gushing with our praise lest the dog gets up because he thinks the exercise is over.

10. The stay exercise is not completed until the dog sits through the praise and remains sitting while we remain standing, upright and relaxed, for a little while longer. Then, we either move on with the dog on the leash after giving the command, "Heel," or we release the dog and encourage him with, "Run along," to move away from us. Even if the dog did not get up until the very end of the stay exercise, we will restart the whole exercise from the beginning. Thus, this exercise has no correction other than a total restart. This links the individual parts of the exercise into a chain of actions for the dog so that he, in the end, will carry out the exercise with great reliability. At the same time we will have learned to stay relaxed when the dog makes a mistake, and to concentrate on the precise execution of all corrections. That, actually, describes precisely what is meant, in dog training, by consistency.

THE RECALL

In order to be successful with our dog in the area of recall, we again need some concentration and a clear understanding as to how to proceed. As has become clear in our discussion of the stay exercise, we must link separate actions into an unchanging sequence. If we insist on the completion of each action, then it will become a ritual for the dog, and in the end he cannot help but complete it. It is more than simple obedience because he does it from an inner need, which means that he likes doing it. Before we discuss the technique of the recall on the model of the recall exercise as it should be incorporated into each walk, let me list the most important rules for the owner's behavior on a walk. It is the walk where we have an opportunity to train ourselves to always proceed in the very same way (i.e., to be consistent).

It is best to train your Rottweiler yourself or have a professional train your dog and then train you how to handle him.

1. On a walk, we should recall our dog only if we really intend to have the dog sit at our left side. If we were to recall our dog without this precise intent, only because we feel he is a bit far away or he could move into a dangerous area, and then were not to bring him all the way to our side, he would soon begin to ignore our calling.

2. The verbal command used for recall can be, for example, "Come." It can be used in conjunction with the dog's name whenever we wish to get the attention of the distracted dog before recalling him. I do not recommend using the dog's name alone as a calling command.

3. In all instances, we give the command, "Come," only once; only in extreme emergencies do we give it twice. Before we give the command, we come to a stop and wait at that spot until the dog is sitting at our left side.

4. If the dog does not come after we have called him once, we will briskly move away in a definite direction. If

we have the chance, we might even hide by stepping behind a tree, a bush, a wall, and silently wait there for the dog. Worried, he will begin looking for us and, in the future, take our calling more seriously, as a warning that says, "Watch out, I am leaving." Then he will come.

5. If we call him several times, the dog will perceive this no longer as a command to come but rather as a constant message that his master is nearby. Why should he come?

6. When the dog is still very young, we will, whenever possible, call him only when he is already coming. Thus our call, "Come," is associated, from the outset, with the corresponding action. We induce the dog to come by running away with excited, overly dramatic movement, then we praise him and, firmly but gently, make him sit at our left side, straighten up and, after a short wait, praise him again.

This procedure is part of the recall exercise that will be explained below. Let's review the essential points of the recall while taking a walk:

Do not recall unless you really want the dog next to you.

Stop and give the command, "Come!" only once.

When the dog comes, always put him on your left side, make him sit, praise him, and then either release him again or put a leash on him.

Without proper obedience training and discipline, your Rottweiler can grow into an unmanageable, overbearing adult.

If the dog does not come, move away without further word, perhaps even hide.

Mistake: Calling the dog while continuing to walk and, when he comes, not insisting on completion of the recall ritual but simply walking on (e.g., while talking with other people).

Bonding is a key component of the pet/owner relationship. It is as vital as supplying the dog with the proper amount of love and care.

If it should happen that the dog is distracted to such a degree that he simply cannot come (play, squirrels, bitch in season, etc.), do not repeat the call but fetch the dog yourself, perhaps using a treat to attract his attention. Neither scold nor praise the dog.

As long as the dog is still very young we will need another person to assist us with the recall exercise, likewise with an adult dog, if he does not stay reliably. Someone must hold him while we walk away. With a dog that has reliably mastered the stay exercise we can work alone.

1. In the area where we usually take our walks, we select a stretch of land that already has something of a channeling effect, that is, it has borders on its sides, such as a little road in the woods, a fire lane, or something similar.

2. After we have told him, "Stay," the dog remains behind—either held back or sitting on his own—while we, without saying another word, walk away. After we have gone 15 to 20 yards, stop, turn around, and face the dog. For about 20 seconds, we stay there in a relaxed motionless stance.

3. Now we say calmly (and without any movement), "Come." The assistant then releases the dog or, respectively, the dog sitting on his own comes. By standing so still we have caused him to grow tense and,

in most cases, he will approach quickly.

When practicing commands, be sure to follow them through to the end.

4. We continue to stand stock-still, relaxed, and saying nothing, and watch from the corners of our eyes where the dog is going. Perhaps he will run past us, but he is more likely to return the less we move.

5. When the dog is close enough, we grab him (still without speaking) by his collar and make him, gently but firmly, sit at our left side. Then we straighten up, stand there relaxed for a second without looking at the dog or turning towards him in any way, and say, "Good dog. Come." Only now is he petted and praised, while he remains in his sit position. If he does not stay in the sit position we treat him as described above.

6. Only now do we take the leash, which we have been carrying around our neck or in a pocket, and attach the snap. Later, we can send the dog away from this position by giving an appropriate command—perhaps, "Go. Run"—while we ourselves remain at this spot until the dog has run off. But at the beginning, we might have

to help him with a little shove, later he will wait expectantly for our command and then run off spontaneously.

7. After we have leashed our dog and before we take our first step to continue our walk, we give him a command such as, "Heel." If we do not do this, our first step will become a visual signal for our dog to continue walking with his master and thus possibly create a misunderstanding in the stay exercise because following the "Stay," we step forward without a word as well. Such little lapses in attention frequently form the basis for an unexpected failure by our dog.

Always be consistent and patient with your Rottweiler during the training process.

PRECISION IS ESSENTIAL

Once again, we have described an apparently simple process, namely the recall, in all details of its structure and its application. Those who might find this too complicated forget that precision and uniformity of our action sequences do not overtax the dog's ability to learn but actually appeal to it. That is to say, that we are giving the dog the opportunity to realize what we wish him to do. And it is exactly this that binds him increasingly to us. Basically, this form of proceeding includes the two elements that are heralded as the Alpha and Omega of dog training in all dog books: consistency and patience. Precision and patience will give our dog the chance to become used to performing a certain chain of actions desired by us until it becomes an inner need for him and he begins to like doing it. This procedure requires a certain amount of effort because we have to prepare ourselves mentally in order to be able to act in a precise manner. If we do make this effort, we are indeed in a position to train our dog all by ourselves on our daily walks with a little bit of concentration and affection, but without spending any additional time, to reliably come on recall and to reliably stay whenever we ask him to do so. Furthermore, by proceeding in such a precise manner, we not only avoid confusing the dog but our interactions with him also make him confident and trusting. This basis of mutual trust will facilitate any more advanced training together. Also, we are now able to keep our dog away from things that he is to stay away from, both inside the house and during the walk. We started this a few days after the dog arrived at our home. But now that he has matured into a juvenile we should return to this aspect of his training.

SETTING TABOOS

A dog feels safe not if we let him get away with everything, but rather when he realizes what he may and may not do. Thus, we will allow him certain freedoms on the one hand, but, on the other hand, set taboos as well. For instance, he is not to enter the kitchen. The trick is to remove the puppy with a forceful shove from the threshold whenever he is about to cross it. In this, the threshold itself plays an important role since dogs, by their nature, respond to visual borders. They also have

A dog feels safe not if we let him get away with everything but rather when he realizes what he may and may not do.

the tendency to accept easily visible border lines, such as the edge of a field. This is also one reason why the sit exercise at the curb is so effective; the edge of the curb will soon trigger an automatic sit. How soon and how permanently the dog will react in the desired manner is only a question of how consistently we execute this exercise.

Training can begin a few days after you bring your Rottweiler pup home. Start with small tasks, such as learning what items in the house are taboo.

We should apply the same calm and relaxed manner that we used to prevent the dog from entering a forbidden room to keep him from jumping onto our best couch. Any action we take will make a stronger impression on the dog (without intimidating him) if we keep our emotions in check. Whenever we allow emotions to control our actions toward our dog, we do harm to the strong bond between us. Acting in a way that is devoid of emotion has the advantage that the dog will not associate our action with our person but rather with the object of his intentions. This can be demonstrated best with a further taboo, a taboo that we must establish so that our Rottweiler will not steal food. Let's assume we have put the grocery bag on the floor and the dog's nose is approaching the package of hot dogs that lies on top and smells so tempting. If, at this very moment, we act decisively, perhaps throwing something like a ringing pot lid onto the floor, then the dog will associate this unexpected and thus frightening event with the object, the hot dog package. When the next similar occasion arises, the hot dogs will remind him of the unpleasant event and he will desist on his own accord.

We should react in a similar way whenever the very young dog grabs for us with his sharp little milk teeth. When the dog gets older and our cry of pain no longer deters him from grabbing us too hard, we calmly tap him on his hard and not very sensitive canine skull. No dog becomes hand-shy if the tap is given at the right moment. In most cases, the dog will now be more careful when grabbing us, and thus we have accomplished our goal. If we provide our dog with a sufficient number of different and interesting toys that he may destroy whenever he feels the desire, he is more likely to leave those objects that are not to be touched alone. In the case of shoes that we have just taken off, watchfulness is called for: they smell so enticingly like us. Thus, we put them where the dog cannot reach them. I recommend doing the same with all items that have a special attraction for our dog.

DISTRACTION MANEUVERS

To keep a young dog from barking constantly is one of the most difficult projects. The best action to take is to distract him, perhaps change his mood by giving him a treat or his favorite toy.

To keep a young dog from barking constantly is a most difficult project, but it can be done.

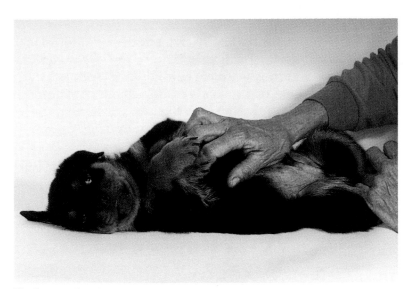

The best action to take against a barking young pup is to distract him. Change his mood by giving him a treat, his favorite toy or a belly rub.

This is a situation where scolding or attempts at calming him are not appropriate, because we will not be able to entirely mask our own nervousness and uncertainty, which will be immediately noticed by the dog, and thus he will increase his barking.

To put an end to the barking and howling of a young dog who has been left alone by himself is even more difficult once he has started it. Thus we should be careful and slow in leaving him by himself. After he has come to feel at home with us, he will also feel more confident in our house and our absence will be less of a burden. Sometimes leaving the radio on will help. And it will surely have a distracting effect if we were to let him have a Nylabone® before we leave. Under no circumstances should we leave timidly because the dog will notice this immediately and become disquieted. We will begin by staying away for short periods only and increase the length of our absences gradually. If, despite this, we do not accomplish our goal, then, unfortunately, we are dealing with a dog that, due to the lack of a varied environment during the first 12 weeks of his life, has not had sufficient opportunity to gain confidence, and we must arm ourselves with patience.

If the dog is afraid of certain noises, we can usually help him best here with a distraction maneuver as well. A treat can work wonders. In the case of explosive sounds as in fireworks, we can transform an adult dog's anxiety into aggression through skillful coaxing, such as, "Watch. Guard." As soon as he stops barking, he will feel stronger and will calm down.

WHEN VISITORS COME

A dog of stable temperament, who as a puppy had enough contact with people, will meet all visitors in a friendly and trusting manner. The worst problem we might have is that he greets our guests too enthusiastically. If, however, he should behave in a reserved manner toward visitors, we should not force him to go up to them. We will ask our guests to ignore the dog for the time being and not to speak to him or pet him until he asks for contact himself. If a dog acts very timidly with visitors, we must not make the mistake of acting insecure ourselves. That will immediately transmit to the dog. With Rottweilers, that as a rule display a pronounced protective behavior, our ambiguous behavior may heighten aggression. Thus we will have to make up our mind whether we will take the risk with our guests and allow the dog in the same room without controlling him, or whether we would rather take him out of the room. However, holding a dog by the collar or on leash in the presence of people who disturb him is the same as intentionally stoking his aggression. The same is true when our dog encounters other dogs.

BASIC TRAINING AND PUBERTY

If we acquired our Rottweiler at age eight to 12 weeks and integrated him sensibly into our family and gave him his basic training, at the half-year mark, we should own an obedient and easy-to-keep dog who, in many respects, appears to understand us well.

All this can change dramatically, although only temporarily, when he enters puberty (i.e., some time between his sixth and seventh month). This process, which leads to the dog's sexual maturity, stresses the animal the same way it stresses people in their adolesence. Up to now, the dog may have executed a number of tasks reliably upon verbal command or hand signal; now he suddenly no longer responds to us and does nothing or the wrong thing. If we think that we must enforce our will because, after all, the dog knows the exercise and what he is to do, we would be making a fundamental error. Dogs do not "know," in the human sense, exactly what they are expected to do. They cannot ascend to this level of consciousness. All we can do is to accustom them to carry out certain actions upon certain verbal and visual signals. Prerequisite is that our signal puts them into the mental state that causes them to perform the desired actions. And that is the one thing that is frequently no longer possible during puberty because their entire emotional state is stressed by the internal processes of change.

It is always important for your dog to know who is in charge, otherwise he will continually test you.

Thus we would be well advised to provide a feeling of security to our Rottweiler rather than take it away by being hardheaded and insistent. Whatever we have accomplished by the time puberty sets in is not lost. Soon we will be able to continue building on that foundation.

ROTTWEILERS as Guardians and Companions

We need not train our Rottweiler to be a guardian, he is one by nature. The more pronounced the protectiveness that he displays for our family, the more he will consider our house or apartment or yard to be an area to which no one but us is granted access. Thus, he will soon begin to report trespassers (i.e., he will bark whenever an unfamiliar person approaches). People who come regularly, such as the mailman, he will soon accept. It would be good if we were to introduce him to such people.

It would be a good idea to introduce your Rottweiler to people who will regularly visit your home, such as close friends and the mailman.

To be sure, we must wait until he is truly grown up for him to demonstrate on his own his talents as guardian. This will usually happen some time between one-and-a-half and two years old; with some dogs it may happen considerably earlier.

Those who cannot wait to have an aggressive watchdog and experiment with their Rottweilers by making them distrustful, or have other non-professionals do it for them, run the risk of trouble. A dog can easily misunderstand us and, if an accident should happen, the owner will be in a real fix. To rehabilitate an animal that has been

Well-socialized Rottweiler puppies learn how to deal with dogs and people alike. A socialized Rottie is the only choice for a guard dog.

made nervous and distrustful into a dog that is calm and confident with people is possible only to a limited degree. Dogs will never totally forget negative experiences. I urgently advise against experiments, especially with Rottweilers. It is entirely sufficient to praise the dog whenever he announces, through barking, the approach of a stranger. If this person is someone who is to be allowed access in the future, we will introduce him to the dog. To that end, we may hand this person a treat to offer the dog.

We must know, however, that the more secure a dog feels in his home territory, the longer he will delay announcing a stranger through barking. Those who spend time with their dogs in a vacation home or camp grounds will easily notice this. Here, in unfamiliar territory, he will be considerably more watchful. Very confident dogs will observe approaching strangers, but will not bark, whereas more timid dogs will

The more secure a dog feels in his home territory the longer he will delay announcing a stranger through barking.

bark much earlier. However, even a confident dog can become less secure in unfamiliar territory and tends to bark sooner.

BARKING ON COMMAND

The most simple and certain method to make a confident dog bark sooner than he would on his own is training him to bark on command. Part of this method is praising him whenever, at any time and for whatever reason, he barks spontaneously, by saying the command, "Speak," in a coaxing voice. The actual training procedure, however, is the following: At a certain spot on our daily walk, we tie the dog with a long leash to a tree or post and then move away without saying a word. We stop after about ten yards, turn around and stand there for a while, relaxed and without moving, facing the dog. This makes the dog tense. Now we move a hand a little, saying at the same time, with our normal speaking voice, "Speak!" As soon as the dog makes the slightest sound, be it whining or the beginning of a bark, we run back to him and give him a treat. Then we walk away again and repeat the exercise two or three times. If the dog should not respond, we will increase the distance gradually or step out of sight behind a tree or bush. Again we will run back to him with praise at his slightest sound.

In order to teach your Rottweiler to bark on command, praise him whenever he barks for any reason.

With a Rottweiler of good temperament, this procedure may be successful at the very first attempt. But it is also possible that there won't be any response at all. In that case, we simply repeat the entire procedure on our next walk at the same spot. After the dog reliably barks on our command, "Speak," (never given more than once) while tied to a tree, we will disconnect the leash from the collar and the next time drop it before walking away. The dog, off lead, will stay behind either standing or sitting. This is a completely new situation for him because he is now under discipline. Barking will be more difficult for him. But we proceed exactly the same way as before. If we are unsuccessful, we will return, without showing any anger, to the on-leash exercise. If this still works, we try again with the dog remaining behind off leash. If we can muster the necessary consistency, we will, with time, surmount the difficulty of having the dog bark while off-leash. We now own a dog who will bark reliably on our command, given only once and in a calm voice, "Speak!" Now we should take advantage of any and all opportunities to make the dog bark in all kinds of different situations until we can make our dog bark whenever someone approaches our house. In the end, the dog will make the association between barking and the appearing of a person, and we have *accomplished* our goal, without allowing the dog to become aggressive. Of course, we will not get angry when, on occasion, the exercise should fail. Scolding would accomplish nothing but make our dog insecure and tense, which makes barking almost impossible for him. We at once return to the first step of the learning process and will reach our goal again very quickly. This step-by-step procedure is

After you have succeeded in teaching your Rottweiler to bark on command while on leash, you may begin to teach it off leash.

applicable and useful for any training objective. With the Rottweiler, we need no more than a warning bark whenever a stranger should show up in the yard or in front of the house. He is an imposing figure to begin with and, if a person should react timidly, he will notice it and be even more on guard.

With a Rottweiler, no more than a warning bark is needed whenever a stranger is in the yard or in front of the house.

Practicing barking on command has the additional advantage that it is now easier to make the dog stop barking whenever his barking is not desired. The prerequisite is that we end each barking exercise with a calmly spoken, "Done!" We will use the very same command when the dog should bark at the wrong time. Additionally, a treat can be helpful in changing the dog's mood, which will make it easier for him to cease barking.

Taking Walks in the Dark

Taking the young dog for a walk at night can be informative. Even in familiar territory, he will behave differently, above all he will be more alert. All sights and sounds clearly affect him more deeply. He will show fear, too, and we should not hold it against him. After all, fear is part of all living beings. A dog who did not know fear would be an underdeveloped creature without any chance of survival in the wild. But a healthy dog with a somewhat even temperament will overcome his fear, mostly because of his curiosity. For instance, he will stop in front of a bush that, lighter than the rest, stands out against the dark background and moves slightly in the wind. His hair will stand on end, he growls, barks, and takes a few steps to the side. For the time being, we should just observe him and neither laugh at him nor support him by urging him on nor attempt to trigger his aggression. In such situations, a dog will frequently try to catch the scent of the object that disquiets him by circling it with his nose held high. Then he will approach and touch and sniff and, finally, mark (by depositing urine) the bush. With that the matter is "closed."

If the dog does not investigate the suspicious object on his own accord, we can help him best by stepping close to it and talking with calming words to the dog and coax him closer. It would be wrong to call him in a harsh voice or pull him closer with the leash. There simply are situations where dogs need some time to adapt. This is especially true during puberty (i.e., approximately from the sixth to the twelfth month). Rather than pressure him, it would be better to return to this frightening situation on another day. If we did not place additional stress on him the first time, he will usually act less afraid.

There is a further option to help a dog who shows fear when confronted with a suspicious apparition: we make him bark with our command, "Speak," that we give in a soft voice and, in this situation, repeat. In doing so we are standing next to the dog, not looking at him but rather, like him, staring at the object in question. Barking always releases some of the dog's tension and soon curiosity will win out and he will investigate the object.

There are situations where dogs need time to adapt. New objects and or new pets can lead to a stress build-up and a need to release tension.

ENCOUNTERS

It is important for a dog's temperament development and his confidence to leave him to his own devices as soon as he is confronted by stressful situations. These include not only phenomena that make him uneasy but also encounters with people that intimidate him (abnormal gait, strange clothing, etc.) and, of no less importance, encounters with other dogs and interactions with them in

By introducing the family cat to your Rottweiler pup, you will allow him to overcome a possible stressful situation early in his life.

Encounters between two energetic puppies can appear alarming. When a play fight escalates to a problem, you will have no difficulty telling.

play or in the measuring ritual or in brawls. In all these situations, owners should not attempt to influence their dogs. This would rob them of the opportunity to learn on their own and to become independent.

If a dog owner were to behave in a fearful manner whenever his dog meets up with another dog, he would, in a way, train his dog to be aggressive. With our robust and powerful Rottweiler we cannot afford to do so. For that reason I am listing here some ideal rules of conduct when meeting other dogs, especially dogs of the same gender. (*Editor's note*: The guidelines herein set forth make perfect canine sense though may *not* be safe with all Rottweilers in all situations. Futher consider local leash laws as well as animal-control regulations before releasing your dog.)

Basic obedience training makes a dog trustworthy in almost any situation. Don't become complacent—practice your commands regularly.

1. Whenever we encounter unrestrained dogs we do not hold back our own with the leash but release him and continue walking, calmly and steadily. To hold him back when meeting other dogs would mean furthering the dog's aggression.

2. Whenever we meet a dog that is being walked on a leash, we keep our dog leashed as well; the leash, however, should hang loosely. When our dog lunges, we pull him forcefully back to our side and immediately loosen the leash again. Through all this we steadily walk on. All dogs are more aggressive when the leash is taut.

3. If we and other dog owners are watching our dogs at the same location and one of the dogs displays aggression by growling or mounting another dog, we will wordlessly walk away several yards and ask the other owners to do the same in divergent directions. To yell loudly at the dogs would at this moment be wrong, at most we will calmly say, "Come."

4. If, despite this, two males or two females should start brawling, we will walk away as before without any other commands than the recall. If we were to rush at the dogs, yell at them or even beat them with leashes or sticks, then the brawl would, without fail, turn into a real fight because our insecurity will transmit itself to the dogs and they will grab harder and, in the end, bite.

5. If it should happen that two dogs have locked jaws and won't let go, we lift up the one on top by his collar. Soon he will not get any air and open his mouth. That is why the other owner must be ready to grab his dog before he attacks his opponent when he lets go. If the other owner should be inexperienced, we must give him the necessary instructions. After the dogs have been separated we must immediately put down the one we lifted by his collar to avoid the danger of strangulation. The owners of the dogs involved should walk away in opposite directions with their dogs off leash.

If we follow these rules without showing our apprehension, the chances are very good that it will not go beyond a brawl which the opponents will end on their own. However, if we were not to follow these rules but rather act hysterically and thoughtlessly, the brawl will, without fail, turn into a real fight that may result in serious injuries.

After a brawl, as well as after hard play, inspect the skin of your dog for small injuries.

After a brawl as well as after hard play we should inspect the skin of our dog for small injuries. These we will thoroughly disinfect.

We must be careful not to identify with our dog when he is involved in play or fights, and not become excited and aggressive ourselves. That would only bring confusion and loss of control. There are people who are unhappy whenever their dog ends up lying under the other dog, after all, they want to own a winner. But it is entirely irrelevant which dog is on top and which on the bottom. The better dog with the steady temperament will reveal himself by not biting nervously and behaving correctly in the canine sense, regardless

Rottweilers must be professionally trained to be attack dogs.

whether he is on top or bottom in play or fight. When playing, the dogs themselves take turns in being on top or bottom.

97

Either must be practiced, and they do this instinctively. We may be very happy with our Rottweiler if he—lying on the bottom beneath his opponent—remains calm until the other finally releases him. Then we know that we own a dog of steady temperament who responds normally.

Leash Training the Young Dog

We may have permitted the puppy and, initially, the young dog as well, to forge forward on the leash, but now the day will come when we have to resolve to teach the dog to respect the leash length and not to pull. When that day arrives depends on the weight and the strength not only of the dog but also of the owner and of those family members who will be handling the dog. We must not wait so long that the dog, pulling on the leash, has become a danger to the person handling him. This is, of course, more likely to be the

A training collar will help greatly in teaching your Rottweiler.

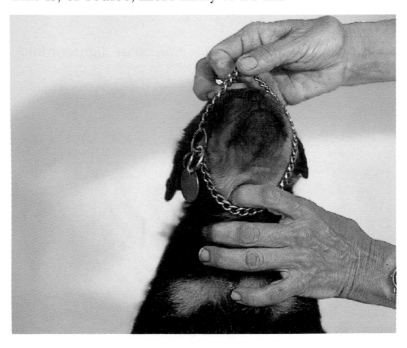

Your Rottweiler pup will quickly become larger than the person handling it. Do not wait long to train your pup; it should be done as early as possible.

case with the compact Rottweiler than with a breed of slighter build. To break him from pulling requires deliberate and not squeamish action. We must clearly understand that our maneuvers must be powerful enough to be immediately effective. If our efforts are too weak, the dog may get used to them, he may even think them to be a game, and our efforts that gradually increase in force, actually train the dog to pull. It is the same here as with giving medicine. The initial dose must be so large that the pathogens cannot adjust to the medication and become resistant. With resistance the medication becomes ineffective.

The procedure: We wait for the young dog to start pulling on the leash. As soon as he does this and the leash is taut, we transport him back with a forceful jerk, by air mail, so to speak. He may go head over heels, but that won't do him any harm, he is robust enough. We do this without any verbal command and keep walking at the same pace. The dog will be bewildered. Often a one-time occurrence will suffice and the dog will have learned that pulling on the leash will result in the unpleasant "return flight." What is unpleasant for the dog is the fact that his forequarters are lifted off the ground. For our correction occurs on an upward slant and at a moment when the taut leash is above his back. Some dogs will attempt again, after a relatively short time, to pull on the leash. If we respond again at the right moment

Your Rottweiler will quickly learn that pulling on the leash will result in the unpleasant "return flight."

with the necessary determination, that should do it for the time being. Now we will be able to observe the dog pushing forward with caution and his inhibition growing as the tension on the leash increases. He will go up to the limit but no further.

Only older dogs who have been taught to pull in the way described above will require more than two repetitions. Any Rottweiler of steady temperament, however, will try again, in the next two days, if he can pull on the leash without being punished. This has to do with how dogs learn. Any experience that impresses a dog will take permanent hold in his memory after two or three days. Only then can we speak of successful learning. Thus, we must not, out of sheer love for our dog, apply corrections that are all too weak when attempting to break our dog from bad habits. That will always make the matter even more for both parties. Dogs, especially Rottweilers, can tolerate

Any correction you are to apply to your Rottweiler should be made clearly, forcefully and without excitement.

a lot, and they will learn quickly when they are corrected at the right moment with the appropriate amount of force. What they do not tolerate is unjustified anger and scolding from their masters because both remain incomprehensible to them, causing confusion. Thus let us apply corrections clearly, forcefully, and without excitement.

The described procedure teaches our Rottweiler to respect the leash length in the sense that he no longer pulls on the leash. This is much more important for everyday dog handling than is correct heeling as it is performed by the obedience dog at dog training class.

BEHAVIOR and Canine Communication

Studies of the human/animal bond point out the importance of the unique relationships that exist between people and their pets. Those of us who share our lives with pets understand the special part they play through companionship, service and protection.

Most likely the majority of our dogs live in family environments. The companionship they provide is well worth the effort involved. In my opinion, every child should have the opportunity to have a family dog. Dogs teach responsibility through understanding their care, feelings and even respecting their life cycles. Frequently those children who have not been exposed to dogs grow up afraid of dogs, which isn't good. Dogs sense timidity and some will take advantage of the situation.

Today more dogs are serving as service dogs. Since the origination of the Seeing Eye dogs years ago, we now have trained hearing dogs. Also dogs are trained to provide service for the handicapped and are able to perform many different tasks for their owners. Search and Rescue dogs, with their handlers, are sent throughout the world to assist in recovery of disaster victims. They are life savers.

CANINE BEHAVIOR

Canine behavior problems are the number-one reason for

In Europe, Rottweilers are used by the police, border patrols and the army for every kind of duty including guarding, searching, attack and camaraderie.

pet owners to dispose of their dogs, either through new homes, humane shelters or euthanasia. Unfortunately there are too many owners who are unwilling to devote the necessary time to properly train their dogs. On the other hand, there are those who not only are concerned about inherited health problems but are also aware of the dog's mental stability.

Unfortunately there are too many owners who are unwilling to devote the necessary time to properly train their Rottweilers.

You may realize that a breed and his group relatives (i.e., sporting, hounds, etc.) show tendencies to behavioral characteristics. An experienced breeder can acquaint you with his breed's personality. Unfortunately many breeds are labeled with poor temperaments when actually the breed as a whole is not affected but only a small percentage of individuals within the breed.

The versatility of the Rottweiler is easily seen by this one clearing the high jump.

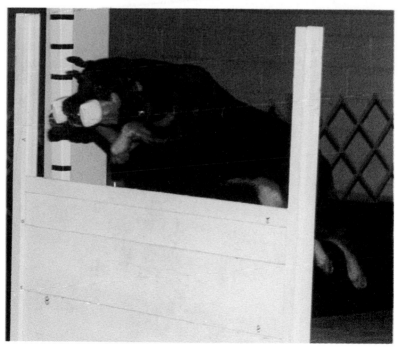

Inheritance and environment contribute to the dog's behavior. Some naïve people suggest inbreeding as the cause of bad temperaments. Inbreeding only results in poor behavior if the ancestors carry the trait. If there are excellent temperaments behind the dogs, then inbreeding will promote good temperaments in the offspring. Did you ever consider that inbreeding is what sets the characteristics of a breed? A purebred dog is the end result of inbreeding. This does not spare the mixed-breed dog from the same problems. Mixed-breed dogs frequently are the offspring of purebred dogs.

Not too many decades ago most of our dogs led a different lifestyle than what is prevalent today. Usually mom stayed home so the dog had human companionship and someone to discipline it if needed. Not much was expected from the dog.

Inheritance and environment contribute to your Rottweiler's behavior.

Today's mom works and everyone's life is at a much faster pace.

The dog may have to adjust to being a "weekend" dog. The family is gone all day during the week, and the dog is left to his own devices for entertainment. Some dogs sleep all day waiting for their family to come home and others become wigwam wreckers if given the opportunity. Crates do ensure the safety of the dog and the house. However, he could become a physically and emotionally cripple if he doesn't get enough exercise and attention. We still appreciate and want the companionship of our dogs although we expect more from them. In many cases we tend to forget dogs are just that—*dogs* not human beings.

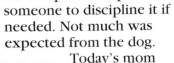

A crate will ensure the safety of your Rottweiler no matter where he is.

It is much easier to start training your Rottweiler puppy before there is a problem that needs to be corrected.

SOCIALIZING AND TRAINING

Many prospective puppy buyers lack experience regarding the proper socialization and training needed to develop the type of pet we all desire. In the first 18 months, training does take some work. Trust me, it is easier to start proper training before there is a problem that needs to be corrected.

The eight- to ten-week age period is a fearful time for puppies. They need to be handled very gently around children and adults. There should be no harsh discipline during this time. Starting at 14 weeks of age, the puppy begins the juvenile period, which ends when he reaches sexual maturity around six to 14 months of age. During the juvenile period he needs to be introduced to strangers (adults, children and other dogs) on the home property. At sexual maturity he will begin to bark at strangers and become more protective. Males start to lift their legs to urinate but if you desire you can inhibit this behavior by walking your boy on leash away from trees, shrubs, fences, etc.

Training includes puppy kindergarten and a minimum of one to two basic training classes. During these classes you will learn how to dominate your youngster. This is especially important if you own a large breed of dog. It is somewhat harder, if not nearly impossible, for some owners to be the Alpha figure when their dog towers over them. You will be taught how to properly restrain your dog. This concept is important. Again it puts you in the Alpha position. All dogs need to be restrained many times during their lives. Believe it or not, some of our worst offenders are the

Accustom your Rottweiler puppy to such grooming procedures as nail trimming and ear cleaning to avoid future problems as an adult.

eight-week-old puppies that are brought to our clinic. They need to be gently restrained for a nail trim but the way they carry on you would think we were killing them. In comparison, their vaccination is a "piece of cake." When we ask dogs to do something that is not agreeable to them, then their worst comes out. Life will be easier for your dog if you expose him at a young age to the necessities of life—proper behavior and restraint.

UNDERSTANDING THE DOG'S LANGUAGE

Most authorities agree that the dog is a descendent of the wolf. The dog and wolf have similar traits. For instance both are pack oriented and prefer not to be isolated for long periods of time. Another characteristic is that the dog, like the wolf, looks to the leader—Alpha—for direction. Both the wolf and the dog communicate through body language, not only within their pack but with outsiders.

Every pack has an Alpha figure. The dog looks to you, or should look to you, to be that leader. If your dog doesn't receive the proper training and guidance, he very well may replace you as Alpha. This would be a serious problem and is certainly a disservice to your dog.

Dogs are popular because of their sociable nature. Those that have contact with humans during the first 12 weeks of life regard them as a member of their own species—their pack. All dogs have the potential for both dominant and submissive behavior. Only through experience and training do they learn to whom it is appropriate to show which behavior. Not all dogs are concerned with dominance but owners need to be aware of that potential. It is wise for the owner to establish his dominance early on.

A human can express dominance or submission toward a dog in the following ways:

1. Meeting the dog's gaze signals dominance. Averting the gaze signals submission. If the dog growls or threatens, averting the gaze is the first avoiding action

Not all Rottweilers are concerned with dominance but owners need to be aware of that potential.

It is wise for an owner to establish his dominance early on in his relationship with his Rottweiler.

to take—it may prevent attack. It is important to establish eye contact in the puppy. The older dog that has not been exposed to eye contact may see it as a threat and will not be willing to submit.

2. Being taller than the dog signals dominance; being lower signals submission. This is why, when attempting to make friends with a strange dog or catch the runaway, one should kneel down to his level. Some owners see their dogs become dominant when allowed on the furniture or on the bed. Then he is at the owner's level.

3. An owner can gain dominance by ignoring all the dog's social initiatives. The owner pays attention to the dog only when he obeys a command.

No dog should be allowed to achieve dominant status over any adult or child. Ways of preventing are as follows:

1. Handle the puppy gently, especially during the three- to four-month period.

2. Let the children and adults handfeed him and teach him to take food without lunging or grabbing.

3. Do not allow him to chase children or joggers.

4. Do not allow him to jump on people or mount their legs. Even females may be inclined to mount. It is not only a male habit.

5. Do not allow him to growl for any reason.

6. Don't participate in wrestling or tug-of-war games.

As much as we would like them to be little people, we must always keep in mind that a dog is a dog and will behave as such.

7. Don't physically punish puppies for aggressive behavior. Restrain him from repeating the infraction and teach an alternative behavior. Dogs should earn everything they receive from their owners. This would include sitting to receive petting or treats, sitting before going out the door and sitting to receive the collar and leash. These types of exercises reinforce the owner's dominance.
Young children should never be left alone with a dog. It is important that children learn some basic obedience commands so they have some control over the dog. They will gain the respect of their dog.

My most important advice to you is to be aware of your dog's actions. Even so, remember dogs are dogs and will behave as such even though we might like them to be perfect little people. You and your dog will become neurotic if you worry about every little indiscretion. When there is reason for concern—don't waste time. Seek guidance. Dogs are meant to be loved and enjoyed.

References:
Manual of Canine Behavior, Valerie O'Farrell, British Small Animal Veterinary Association.
Good Owners, Great Dogs, Brian Kilcommons, Warner Books.

It is important that children learn some basic obedience commands so they have some control over the dog.

TRAVELING with Your Dog

The earlier you start traveling with your new puppy or dog, the better. He needs to become accustomed to traveling. However, some dogs are nervous riders and become carsick easily. It is helpful if he starts with an empty stomach. Do not despair, as it will go better if you continue taking him with you on short fun rides. How would you feel if every time you rode in the car you stopped at the doctor's for an injection? You would soon dread that nasty car. Older dogs that tend to get carsick may have more of a problem adjusting to traveling. Those dogs that are having a serious problem may benefit from some medication prescribed by the veterinarian.

Do give your dog a chance to relieve himself before getting into the car. It is a good idea to be prepared for a clean up with a leash, paper towels, bag and terry cloth towel.

The safest place for your dog is in a fiberglass crate, although close confinement can promote carsickness in some dogs. If your dog is nervous you can try letting him ride on the seat next to you or in someone's lap.

An alternative to the crate would be to use a car harness made for dogs and/or a safety strap attached to the harness

Traveling crates can provide safe and easy transport for your dog. Ventilation for travel is a most important consideration.

or collar. Whatever you do, do not let your dog ride in the back of a pickup truck unless he is securely tied on a very short lead. I've seen trucks stop quickly and, even though the dog was tied, it fell out and was dragged.

I do occasionally let my dogs ride loose with me because I really enjoy their companionship, but in all honesty they are safer in their crates. I have a friend whose van rolled in an accident but his dogs, in their fiberglass crates, were not injured nor did they escape. Another advantage of the crate is that it is a safe place to leave him if you need to run into the store. Otherwise you wouldn't be able to leave the windows down. Keep in mind that while many dogs are overly protective in their crates, this may not be enough to deter dognappers. In some states it is against the law to leave a dog in the car unattended.

There are many safe means available of traveling with your pets, one of which is not carrying them in a basket.

Never leave a dog loose in the car wearing a collar and leash. I have known more than one dog that has killed himself by hanging. Do not let him put his head out an open window. Foreign debris can be blown into his eyes. When leaving your dog unattended in a car, consider the temperature. It can take less than five minutes to reach temperatures over 100 degrees.

In a reputable boarding kennel your Rottweiler will have stimulation from other dogs as well as people.

TRIPS

Perhaps you are taking a trip. Give consideration to what is best for your dog—traveling with you or boarding. When traveling by car, van or motor home, you need to think ahead about locking your vehicle. In all probability you have many valuables in the car and do not wish to leave it unlocked. Perhaps most valuable and not replaceable is your dog. Give thought to securing your vehicle and providing adequate ventilation for him. Another consideration for you when traveling with your dog is medical problems that may arise and little inconveniences, such as exposure to external parasites. Some areas of the country are quite flea infested. You may want to carry flea spray with you. This is even a good idea when staying in motels. Quite possibly you are not the only occupant of the room.

Unbelievably many motels and even hotels do allow canine guests, even some very first-class ones. Gaines Pet Foods Corporation publishes *Touring With Towser*, a directory of domestic hotels and motels that accommodate guests

Four Paws Pet Safety Sitter is designed to protect pets from injury by securing them in place and preventing them from disturbing drivers and passengers.

with dogs. Their address is Gaines TWT, PO Box 5700, Kankakee, IL, 60902. I would recommend you call ahead to any motel that you may be considering and see if they accept pets. Sometimes it is necessary to pay a deposit against room damage. Of course you are more likely to gain accommodations for a small dog than a large dog. Also the management feels reassured when you mention that your dog will be crated. Since my dogs tend to bark when I leave the room, I leave the TV on nearly full blast to deaden the noises outside that tend to encourage my dogs to bark. If you do travel with your dog, take along plenty of baggies so that you can clean up after him. When we all do our share in cleaning up, we make it possible for motels to continue accepting our pets. As a matter of fact, you should practice cleaning up everywhere you take your dog.

Depending on where your are traveling, you may need an up-to-date health certificate issued by your veterinarian. It is good policy to take along your dog's medical information, which would include the name, address and phone number of your veterinarian, vaccination record, rabies certificate, and any medication he is taking.

AIR TRAVEL

When traveling by air, you need to contact the airlines to check their policy. Usually you have to make arrangements up to a couple of weeks in advance for traveling with your dog. The airlines require your dog to travel in an airline approved fiberglass crate. Usually these can be purchased through the airlines but they are also readily available in most pet-supply stores. If your dog is not accustomed to a crate, then it is a good idea to get him acclimated to it before your trip. The day of the actual trip you should withhold water about one hour ahead of departure and no food for about 12 hours. The airlines generally have temperature restrictions, which do not allow pets to travel if it is either too cold or too hot. Frequently these restrictions are based on the temperatures at the departure and arrival airports. It's best to inquire about a health certificate. These usually need to be issued within ten days of departure. You should arrange for non-stop, direct flights and if a commuter plane should be involved, check to see if it will carry dogs. Some don't. The

Humane Society of the United States has put together a tip sheet for airline traveling. You can receive a copy by sending a self-addressed stamped envelope to:

The Humane Society of the United States
Tip Sheet
2100 L Street NW
Washington, DC 20037.

Regulations differ for traveling outside of the country and are sometimes changed without notice. Well in advance you need to write or call the appropriate consulate or agricultural department for instructions. Some countries have lengthy quarantines (six months), and countries differ in their rabies vaccination requirements. For instance, it may have to be given at least 30 days ahead of your departure.

If you are planning to have your puppy shipped from across the country or overseas, find out all the necessary regulations.

Do make sure your dog is wearing proper identification. You never know

when you might be in an accident and separated from your dog. Or your dog could be frightened and somehow manage to escape and run away. When I travel, my dogs wear collars with engraved nameplates with my name, phone number and city.

Another suggestion would be to carry in-case-of-emergency instructions. These would include the address and phone number of a relative or friend, your veterinarian's name, address and phone number, and your dog's medical information.

BOARDING KENNELS

Perhaps you have decided that you need to board your dog. Your veterinarian can recommend a good boarding facility or possibly a pet sitter that will come to your house. It is customary for the boarding kennel to ask for proof of vaccination for the DHLPP, rabies and bordetella vaccine. The bordetella should have been given within six months of boarding. This is for your protection. If they do not ask for this proof I would not board at their kennel. Ask about flea control. Those dogs that suffer flea-bite allergy can get in trouble at a boarding kennel. Unfortunately boarding kennels are limited on how much they are able to do.

For more information on pet sitting, contact NAPPS:
National Association of Professional Pet Sitters
1200 G Street, NW
Suite 760
Washington, DC 20005.

Boarding kennels are usually equipped with outdoor runs that offer shelter from the elements.

Our clinic has technicians that pet sit and technicians that board clinic patients in their homes. This may be an alternative for you. Ask your veterinarian if they have an employee that can help you. There is a definite advantage of having a technician care for your dog, especially if your dog is on medication or is a senior citizen.

Some veterinary technicians provide home-boarding services. Check with your vet to see if any of his staff does.

You can write for a copy of *Traveling With Your Pet* from ASPCA, Education Department, 441 E. 92nd Street, New York, NY 10128.

It is smart to investigate everything about the boarding facility you are choosing so as not to worry about the safety of your pet.

IDENTIFICATION and Finding the Lost Dog

There are several ways of identifying your dog. The old standby is a collar with dog license, rabies, and ID tags. Unfortunately collars have a way of being separated from the dog and tags fall off. I am not suggesting you shouldn't use a collar and tags. If they stay intact and on the dog, they are the quickest way of identification.

For several years owners have been tattooing their dogs. Some tattoos use a number with a registry. Here lies the problem because there are several registries to check. If you wish to tattoo, use your social security number. The humane shelters have the means to trace it. It is usually done on the inside of the rear thigh. The area is first shaved and numbed. There is no pain, although a few dogs do not like the buzzing sound. Occasionally tattooing is not legible and needs to be redone.

The newest method of identification is microchipping. The microchip is a computer chip that is no larger than a grain of rice. The veterinarian implants it by injection between the shoulder blades. The dog feels no discomfort. If your dog is lost and picked up by the humane society, they can trace you by scanning the microchip, which has its own code. Microchip scanners are friendly to other brands of microchips and their registries. The microchip comes with a dog tag saying the dog is microchipped. It is the safest way of identifying your dog.

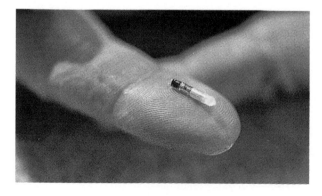

A microchip implant comes in handy should your Rotty get lost. These are easy for veterinarians to implant and prove invaluable should you lose your pet.

FINDING THE LOST DOG

I am sure you will agree with me that there would be little worse than losing your dog. Responsible pet owners rarely lose their dogs. They do not let their dogs run free because they don't want harm to come to them. Not only that but in most, if not all, states there is a leash law.

Losing your pet Rottweiler would be devastating to you as well as your family. Responsibility in ownership is the only way to guarantee the safety of your pet.

Beware of fenced-in yards. They can be a hazard. Dogs find ways to escape either over or under the fence. Another fast exit is through the gate that perhaps the neighbor's child left unlocked.

Below is a list that hopefully will be of help to you if you need it. Remember don't give up, keep looking. Your dog is worth your efforts.

1. Contact your neighbors and put flyers with a photo on it in their mailboxes. Information you should include would be the dog's name, breed, sex, color, age, source of identification, when your dog was last seen and where, and your name and phone numbers. It may be helpful to say the dog needs medical care. Offer a *reward*.

2. Check all local shelters daily. It is also possible for your dog to be picked up away from home and end up in an out-of-the-way shelter. Check these too. Go in person. It is not good enough to call. Most shelters are limited on the time they can hold dogs then they are put up for adoption or euthanized. There is the possibility that your dog will not make it to the shelter for several days. Your dog could have been wandering or someone may have tried to keep him.

3. Notify all local veterinarians. Call and send flyers.

4. Call your breeder. Frequently breeders are contacted when one of their breed is found.

5. Contact the rescue group for your breed.

6. Contact local schools—children may have seen your dog.

7. Post flyers at the schools, groceries, gas stations, convenience stores, veterinary clinics, groomers and any other place that will allow them.

8. Advertise in the newspaper.

9. Advertise on the radio.

SPORT of Purebred Dogs

Welcome to the exciting and sometimes frustrating sport of dogs. No doubt you are trying to learn more about dogs or you wouldn't be deep into this book. This section covers the basics that may entice you, further your knowledge and help you to understand the dog world. If you decide to give showing, obedience or any other dog activities a try, then I suggest you seek further help from the appropriate source.

Agility is an obstacle course designed to test a dog's intelligence and coordination.

Dog showing has been a very popular sport for a long time and has been taken quite seriously by some. Others only enjoy it as a hobby.

The Kennel Club in England was formed in 1859, the American Kennel Club was established in 1884 and the Canadian Kennel Club was formed in 1888. The purpose of these clubs was to register purebred dogs and maintain their Stud Books. In the beginning, the concept of registering dogs was not readily accepted. More than 36 million dogs have been enrolled in the AKC Stud Book since its inception in 1888. Presently the kennel clubs not only register dogs but adopt and enforce rules and regulations governing dog shows, obedience trials and field trials. Over the years they have fostered and encouraged interest in the health and welfare of the purebred dog. They routinely donate funds to veterinary research for study on genetic disorders.

Below are the addresses of the kennel clubs in the United States, Great Britain and Canada.

The American Kennel Club
51 Madison Avenue
New York, NY 10010
(Their registry is located at: 5580 Centerview Drive, STE 200, Raleigh, NC 27606-3390)

The Kennel Club
1 Clarges Street
Piccadilly, London, WIY 8AB, England

The Canadian Kennel Club
111 Eglinton Avenue
East Toronto, Ontario M6S 4V7
Canada

Today there are numerous activities that are enjoyable for both the dog and the handler. Some of the activities include conformation showing, obedience competition, agility, the Canine Good Citizen Certificate, and a wide range of instinct tests that vary from breed to breed. Where you start depends upon your goals which early on may not be readily apparent.

CONFORMATION
Conformation showing is our oldest dog show sport. This type of showing is based on the dog's appearance— that is his structure, movement and attitude. When considering this type of showing, you need to be aware of your breed's standard and be able to evaluate your dog compared to that standard. The breeder of your puppy or other experienced breeders would be good sources for such an evaluation. Puppies can go through lots of changes over a period of time. I always say most puppies start out as promising hopefuls and then after maturing

Conformation showing is our oldest dog show sport. It is based on the dog's appearance— his structure, movement and attitude.

may be disappointing as show candidates. Even so this should not deter them from being excellent pets.

Usually conformation training classes are offered by the local kennel or obedience clubs. These are excellent places for training puppies. The puppy should be able to walk on a lead before entering such a class. Proper ring procedure and technique for posing (stacking) the dog will be demonstrated as well as gaiting the dog. Usually certain patterns

It takes time to learn the routine of conformation showing. Conformation training classes are offered by the local kennel or obedience clubs.

are used in the ring such as the triangle or the "L." Conformation class, like the PKT class, will give your youngster the opportunity to socialize with different breeds of dogs and humans too.

It takes some time to learn the routine of conformation showing. Usually one starts at the puppy matches which may be AKC Sanctioned or Fun Matches. These matches are generally for puppies from two or three months to a year old, and there may be classes for the adult over the age of 12 months. Similar to point shows, the classes are divided by sex and after completion of the classes in that breed or variety, the class winners compete for Best of Breed or Variety. The winner goes on to compete in the Group and the Group winners compete for Best in Match. No championship points are awarded for match wins.

A few matches can be great training for puppies even though there is no intention to go on showing. Matches enable the puppy to meet new people and be handled by a stranger—the judge. It is also a change of environment, which broadens the horizon for both dog and handler. Matches and other dog activities boost the confidence of the handler and especially the younger handlers.

Earning an AKC championship is built on a point system, which is different from Great Britain. To become an AKC Champion of Record the dog must earn 15 points. The number of points earned each time depends upon the number of dogs in competition. The number of points available at each show depends upon the breed, its sex and the location of the show. The United States is divided into ten AKC zones. Each zone has its own set of points. The purpose of the zones is to try to equalize the points available from breed to breed and area to area. The AKC adjusts the point scale annually.

The number of points that can be won at a show are between one and five. Three-, four- and five-point wins are considered majors. Not only does the dog need 15 points won under three different judges, but those points must include two majors under two different judges. Canada also works on a point system but majors are not required.

Practice stacking your Rottweiler at all times, as if you were in competition, and the dog will quickly become accustomed to the procedure.

Junior Showmanship

The Junior Showmanship Class is a wonderful way to build self

confidence even if there are no aspirations of staying with the dog-show game later in life. Frequently, Junior Showmanship becomes the background of those who become successful exhibitors/handlers in the future. In some instances it is taken very seriously, and success is measured in terms of wins. The Junior Handler is judged solely on his ability and skill in presenting his dog. The dog's conformation is not to be considered by the judge. Even so the condition and grooming of the dog may be a reflection upon the handler.

Canine Good Citizen

The AKC sponsors a program to encourage dog owners to train their dogs. Local clubs perform the pass/fail tests, and dogs who pass are awarded a Canine Good Citizen Certificate. Proof of vaccination is required at the time of participation. The test includes:

Canine Good Citizen is a program sponsored by the AKC to encourage dog owners to train their dogs.

1. Accepting a friendly stranger.
2. Sitting politely for petting.
3. Appearance and grooming.
4. Walking on a loose leash.
5. Walking through a crowd.
6. Sit and down on command/staying in place.
7. Come when called.
8. Reaction to another dog.
9. Reactions to distractions.
10. Supervised separation.

If more effort was made by pet owners to accomplish these exercises, fewer dogs would be cast off to the humane shelter.

Obedience

Obedience is necessary, without a doubt, but it can also become a wonderful hobby or even an obsession. In my opinion, obedience classes and competition can provide wonderful companionship, not only with your dog but with your classmates or fellow competitors. It is always gratifying

This Rottweiler is clearing the broad jump in open obedience. U.S. The AKC acknowledged agility in August 1994. Dogs must be at least 12 months of age to be entered. It is a fascinating sport that the dog, handler and spectators enjoy to the utmost. Agility is a spectator sport! The dog performs off lead. The handler either runs with his dog or positions himself on the course and directs his dog with verbal and hand signals over a timed course over or through a variety of obstacles including a time out or pause. One of the main drawbacks to agility is finding a place to train. The obstacles take up a lot of space and it is very time consuming to put up and take down courses.

The titles earned at AKC agility trials are Novice Agility Dog (NAD), Open Agility Dog (OAD), Agility Dog Excellent (ADX), and Master Agility Excellent (MAX). In order to acquire an agility title, a dog must earn a qualifying score in its respective class on three separate occasions under two different judges. The MAX will be awarded after earning ten qualifying scores in the Agility Excellent Class.

PERFORMANCE TESTS

During the last decade the American Kennel Club has promoted performance tests—those events that test the different breeds' natural abilities. This type of event encourages a handler to devote even more time to his dog and retain the natural instincts of his breed heritage. It is an important part of the wonderful world of dogs.

Herding Titles

For all Herding breeds and Rottweilers and Samoyeds.

Entrants must be at least nine months of age and dogs with limited registration (ILP) are eligible. The Herding program is divided into Testing and Trial sections. The goal is to demonstrate proficiency in herding livestock in diverse situations. The titles offered are Herding Started (HS), Herding Intermediate (HI), and Herding Excellent (HX). Upon completion of the HX a Herding Championship may be earned after accumulating 15 championship points.

Schutzhund is a fast growing competitive sport in the United States and has been popular in England since the early 1900s.

The above information has been taken from the AKC Guidelines for the appropriate events.

SCHUTZHUND

The German word "Schutzhund" translated to English means "Protection Dog." It is a fast growing competitive sport in the United States and has been popular in England since the early 1900s. Schutzhund was originally a test to determine which German Shepherds were quality dogs for breeding in Germany. It gives us the ability to test our dogs

131

for correct temperament and working ability. Like every other dog sport, it requires teamwork between the handler and the dog.

Schutzhund training and showing involves three phases: Tracking, Obedience and Protection. There are three SchH levels: SchH I (novice), SchH II (intermediate), and SchH III (advanced). Each title becomes progressively more difficult. The handler and dog start out in each phase with 100 points. Points are deducted as errors are incurred. A total perfect score is 300, and for a dog and handler to earn a title he must earn at least 70 points in tracking and obedience and at least 80 points in protection. Today many different breeds participate successfully in Schutzhund.

This Rottweiler is in a weight pull competition. Only dogs that have mastered obedience should be trained for this type of competition.

GENERAL INFORMATION

Obedience, tracking and agility allow the purebred dog with an Indefinite Listing Privilege (ILP) number or a limited registration to be exhibited and earn titles. Application must be made to the AKC for an ILP number.

The American Kennel Club publishes a monthly *events* magazine that is part of the *Gazette*, their official journal for the sport of purebred dogs. The *Events* section lists upcoming shows and the secretary or superintendent for them. The majority of the conformation shows in the U.S. are overseen by licensed superintendents. Generally the entry closing date is approximately two-and-a-half weeks before the actual show. Point shows are fairly expensive, while the match shows cost about one third of the point show entry fee. Match shows usually take

There are numerous activities you and your Rottweiler can do together. Your dog can only benefit from your attention and training.

entries the day of the show but some are pre-entry. The best way to find match show information is through your local kennel club. Upon asking, the AKC can provide you with a list of superintendents, and you can write and ask to be put on their mailing lists.

Obedience trial and tracking test information is available through the AKC. Frequently these events are not superintended, but put on by the host club. Therefore you would make the entry with the event's secretary.

As you have read, there are numerous activities you can share with your dog. Regardless what you do, it does take teamwork. Your dog can only benefit from your attention and training. I hope this chapter has enlightened you and hope, if nothing else, you will attend a show here and there. Perhaps you will start with a puppy kindergarten class, and who knows where it may lead!

HEALTH CARE for Your Rottweiler

Veterinary medicine has become far more sophisticated than what was available to our ancestors. This can be attributed to the increase in household pets and consequently the demand for better care for them. Also human medicine has become far more complex. *Your pet Rottweiler can only benefit from regular check ups.* Today diagnostic testing in veterinary medicine parallels human diagnostics. Because of better technology we can expect our pets to live healthier lives thereby increasing their life spans.

THE FIRST CHECK UP

You will want to take your new puppy/dog in for its first check up within 48 to 72 hours after acquiring it. Many breeders strongly recommend this check up and so do the humane shelters. A puppy/dog can appear healthy but it may have a serious problem that is not apparent to the layman. Most pets have some type of a minor flaw that may never cause a real problem.

Unfortunately if he/she should have a serious problem, you will want to consider the consequences of keeping the pet and the attachments that will be formed, which may be broken prematurely. Keep in mind there are many healthy dogs looking for good homes.

This first check up is a good time to establish yourself with the veterinarian and learn the office policy regarding their hours and how they handle emergencies. Usually the breeder or another conscientious pet owner is a good reference for locating a capable veterinarian. You should be aware that not all veterinarians give the same quality of service. Please do not make your selection on the least expensive clinic, as they may be short changing your pet. There is the possibility that eventually it will cost you more due to improper diagnosis, treatment, etc. If you are selecting a new veterinarian, feel free to ask for a tour of the clinic. You should inquire about

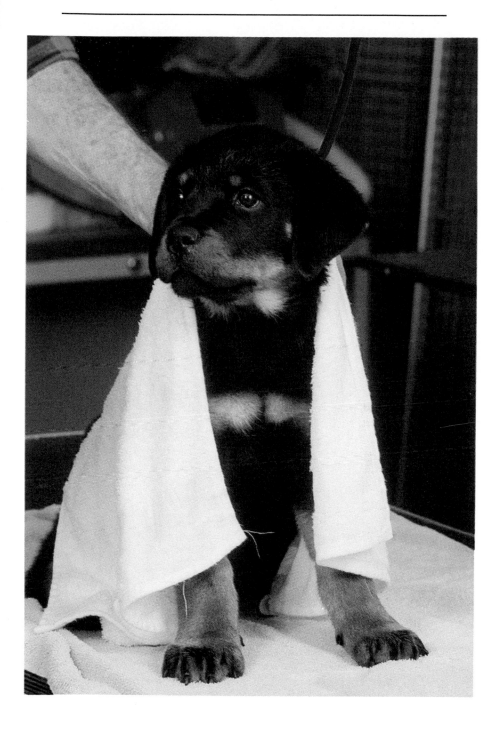

A tour of the veterinary clinic will give you ease of mind should your Rottie become ill and require attention. Be sure the accommodations are safe and sanitary.

making an appointment for a tour since all clinics are working clinics, and therefore may not be available all day for sightseers. You may worry less if you see where your pet will be spending the day if he ever needs to be hospitalized.

THE PHYSICAL EXAM

Your veterinarian will check your pet's overall condition, which includes listening to the heart; checking the respiration; feeling the abdomen, muscles and joints; checking the mouth, which includes the gum color and signs of gum disease along with plaque buildup; checking the ears for signs of an infection or ear mites; examining the eyes; and, last but not least, checking the condition of the skin and coat.

He should ask you questions regarding your pet's eating and elimination habits and invite you to relay your questions. It is a good idea to prepare a list so as not to forget anything. He should discuss the proper diet and the quantity to be fed. If this should differ from your breeder's recommendation, then you should convey to him the breeder's choice and see if he approves. If he recommends changing the diet, then this should be done over a few days so as not to cause a gastrointestinal upset. It is customary to take in a fresh stool sample (just a small amount) for a test for intestinal parasites. It must be fresh, preferably within 12 hours, since the eggs hatch quickly and after hatching will not be observed under the microscope. If your pet isn't obliging then, usually the technician can take one in the clinic.

Most lab tests are performed right in your own veterinary office and results are usually made available on the same day.

IMMUNIZATIONS

It is important that you take your puppy/dog's vaccination record with you on your first visit. In case of a puppy, presumably the breeder has seen to the vaccinations up to the time you acquired custody. Veterinarians differ in their vaccination protocol. It is not unusual for your puppy to have received vaccinations for distemper, hepatitis, leptospirosis, parvovirus and parainfluenza every two to three weeks from the age of five or six weeks. Usually this is a combined injection and is typically called the DHLPP. The DHLPP is given through at least 12 to 14 weeks of age, and it is customary to continue with another parvovirus vaccine at 16 to 18 weeks. You may wonder why so many immunizations are necessary. No one knows for sure when the puppy's maternal antibodies are gone, although it is customarily accepted that distemper antibodies are gone by 12 weeks. Usually parvovirus antibodies are gone by 16 to 18 weeks of age. However, it is possible for the maternal antibodies to be gone at a much earlier age or even a later age. Therefore immunizations are started at an early age. The vaccine will not give immunity as long as there are maternal antibodies.

The rabies vaccination is given at three or six months of age depending on your local laws. A vaccine for bordetella (kennel cough) is advisable and can be given anytime from the age of five weeks. The coronavirus is not commonly given unless there is a problem locally. The Lyme vaccine is necessary in endemic areas. Lyme disease has been reported in 47 states.

Distemper

This is virtually an incurable disease. If the dog recovers, he is subject to severe nervous disorders. The virus attacks every tissue in the body and resembles a bad cold with a fever. It can cause a runny nose and eyes and

Your Rottweiler puppy should be vaccinated against distemper starting at six to eight weeks of age.

cause gastrointestinal disorders, including a poor appetite, vomiting and diarrhea. The virus is carried by raccoons, foxes, wolves, mink and other dogs. Unvaccinated youngsters and senior citizens are very susceptible. This is still a common disease.

Hepatitis

This is a virus that is most serious in very young dogs. It is spread by contact with an infected animal or its stool or urine. The virus affects the liver and kidneys and is characterized by high fever, depression and lack of appetite. Recovered animals may be afflicted with chronic illnesses.

Leptospirosis

This is a bacterial disease transmitted by contact with the urine of an infected dog, rat or other wildlife. It produces severe symptoms of fever, depression, jaundice and internal bleeding and was fatal before the vaccine was developed. Recovered dogs can be carriers, and the disease can be transmitted from dogs to humans.

Parvovirus

This was first noted in the late 1970s and is still a fatal disease. However, with proper vaccinations, early diagnosis and prompt treatment, it is a manageable disease. It attacks the bone marrow and intestinal tract. The symptoms include depression, loss of appetite, vomiting, diarrhea and collapse. Immediate medical attention is of the essence.

Rabies

This is shed in the saliva and is carried by raccoons, skunks, foxes, other dogs and cats. It attacks nerve tissue, resulting in paralysis and death. Rabies can be transmitted to people and is virtually always fatal. This disease is reappearing in the suburbs.

Bordetella (Kennel Cough)

The symptoms are coughing, sneezing, hacking and retching accompanied by nasal discharge usually lasting from a few days to several weeks. There are several disease-producing organisms responsible for this disease. The present vaccines are helpful but do not protect for all the strains. It usually is not life threatening but in some instances it can progress to a serious bronchopneumonia. The disease is highly contagious. The vaccination should be given routinely for dogs that come in contact with other dogs, such as through boarding, training class or visits to the groomer.

Coronavirus

This is usually self limiting and not life threatening. It was first noted in the late '70s about a year before parvovirus. The virus produces a yellow/brown

Lyme disease is most often acquired by the parasitic bite of an infected deer tick.

stool and there may be depression, vomiting and diarrhea.

Lyme Disease

This was first diagnosed in the United States in 1976 in Lyme, CT in people who lived in close proximity to the deer tick. Symptoms may include acute lameness, fever, swelling of joints and loss of appetite. Your veterinarian can advise you if you live in an endemic area.

After your puppy has completed his puppy vaccinations, you will continue to booster the DHLPP once a year. It is customary to booster the rabies one year after the first vaccine and then, depending on where you live, it should be boostered every year or every three years. This depends on your local laws. The Lyme and corona vaccines are boostered annually and it is recommended that the bordetella be boostered every six to eight months.

ANNUAL VISIT

I would like to impress the importance of the annual check up, which would include the booster vaccinations, check for intestinal parasites and test for heartworm. Today in our very busy world it is rush, rush and see "how much you can get for how little." Unbelievably, some non-veterinary businesses have entered into the vaccination business. More harm than good can come to your dog through improper vaccinations, possibly from inferior vaccines and/or the wrong schedule. More than likely you truly care about your companion dog and over the years you have devoted much time and expense to his well being. Perhaps you are unaware that a vaccination is not just a vaccination. There is more involved. Please, please follow through with regular physical examinations. It is so important for your veterinarian to know your dog and this is especially true during middle age through the geriatric years. More than likely your older dog will require more than one physical a year. The annual physical is good preventive medicine. Through early diagnosis and subsequent treatment your dog can maintain a longer and better quality of life.

An annual physical is good preventive medicine. It helps to keep your veterinarian aware of your dog's personality and records.

INTESTINAL PARASITES

Hookworms

These are an almost microscopic intestinal worms that can cause anemia and therefore serious problems, including death, in young puppies. Hookworms can be transmitted to humans through penetration of the skin. Puppies may be born with them.

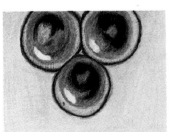

Roundworm eggs as would be seen on a fecal evaluation. The eggs must develop for at least 12 days before they are infective.

Roundworms

These are spaghetti-like worms that can cause a potbellied appearance and dull coat along with more severe symptoms, such as vomiting, diarrhea and coughing. Puppies acquire these while in the mother's uterus and through lactation. Both hookworms and roundworms may be acquired through ingestion.

Whipworms

These have a three-month life cycle and are not acquired through the dam. They cause intermittent diarrhea usually with mucus. Whipworms are possibly the most difficult worm to eradicate. Their eggs are very resistant to most environmental factors and can last for years until the proper conditions enable them to mature. Whipworms are seldom seen in the stool.

Whipworms are hard to find unless one strains the feces, and this is best left to a veterinarian. Pictured here are adult whipworms.

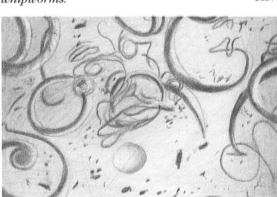

Intestinal parasites are more prevalent in some areas than others. Climate, soil and contamination are big factors contributing to the incidence of intestinal parasites. Eggs are passed in the stool, lay on the ground and then become infective in a certain number of days. Each of the above worms has a different life cycle. Your best chance of becoming and remaining worm-free is to always pooper-scoop your yard. A fenced-in yard keeps stray dogs out, which is certainly helpful.

I would recommend having a fecal examination on your dog twice a year or more often if there is a problem. If your dog has a positive fecal sample, then he will be given the appropriate medication and you will be asked to bring back

another stool sample in a certain period of time (depending on the type of worm) and then be rewormed. This process goes on until he has at least two negative samples. The different types of worms require different medications. You will be wasting your money and doing your dog an injustice by buying over-the-counter medication without first consulting your veterinarian.

OTHER INTERNAL PARASITES

Coccidiosis and Giardiasis

These protozoal infections usually affect puppies, especially in places where large numbers of puppies are brought together. Older dogs may harbor these infections but do not show signs unless they are stressed. Symptoms include diarrhea, weight loss and lack of appetite. These infections are not always apparent in the fecal examination.

Tapeworms

Seldom apparent on fecal floatation, they are diagnosed frequently as rice-like segments around the dog's anus and the base of the tail. Tapeworms are long, flat and ribbon like, sometimes several feet in length, and made up of many segments about five-eighths of an inch long. The two most common types of tapeworms found in the dog are:

(1) First the larval form of the flea tapeworm parasite must mature in an intermediate host, the flea, before it can become infective. Your dog acquires this by ingesting the flea through licking and chewing.

(2) Rabbits, rodents and certain large game animals serve as intermediate hosts for other species of tapeworms. If your dog should eat one of these infected hosts, then he can acquire tapeworms.

HEARTWORM DISEASE

This is a worm that resides in the heart and adjacent blood vessels of the lung that produces microfilaria, which circulate in the bloodstream. It is possible for a dog to be infected with any number of worms from one to a hundred that can be 6 to 14 inches long. It is a life-threatening disease, expensive to treat and easily prevented. Depending on where you live, your veterinarian may recommend a

Most dogs have allergic reactions to flea bites. These pests prove to be your dog's worst enemy.

preventive year-round and either an annual or semiannual blood test. The most common preventive is given once a month.

EXTERNAL PARASITES

Fleas

These pests are not only the dog's worst enemy but also enemy to the owner's pocketbook. Preventing is less expensive than treating, but regardless I think we'd prefer to spend our money elsewhere. I would guess

Preventing fleas is far less expensive than treatment. Give your Rottweiler's coat a thorough going over daily to avoid a problem.

If your Rottweiler puppy or adult does become infected with fleas, there are several good flea baths available on the market.

that the majority of our dogs are allergic to the bite of a flea, and in many cases it only takes one flea bite. The protein in the flea's saliva is the culprit. Allergic dogs have a reaction, which usually

results in a "hot spot." More than likely such a reaction will involve a trip to the veterinarian for treatment. Yes, prevention is less expensive. Fortunately today there are several good products available.

If there is a flea infestation, no one product is going to correct the problem. Not only will the dog require treatment so will the environment. In general flea collars are not very effective although there is now available an "egg" collar that will kill the eggs on the dog. Dips are the most economical but they are messy. There are some effective shampoos and treatments available through pet shops and veterinarians. An oral tablet arrived on the American market in 1995 and was popular in Europe the previous year. It sterilizes the female flea but will not kill adult fleas. Therefore the tablet, which is given monthly, will decrease the flea population but is not a "cure-all." Those dogs that suffer from flea-bite allergy will still be subjected to the bite of the flea. Another popular parasiticide is permethrin, which is applied to the back of the dog in one or two places depending on the dog's weight. This product works as a repellent causing the flea to get "hot feet" and jump off. Do not confuse this product with some of the organophosphates that are also applied to the dog's back.

Some products are not usable on young puppies. Treating fleas should be done under your veterinarian's guidance. Frequently it is necessary to combine products and the layman does not have the knowledge regarding possible toxicities. It is hard to believe but there are a few

Your dog is not the only one that will require treatment should a flea infestation arise. His bed, your house and yard must be treated as well.

dogs that do have a natural resistance to fleas. Nevertheless it would be wise to treat all pets at the same time. Don't forget your cats. Cats just love to prowl the neighborhood and consequently return with unwanted guests.

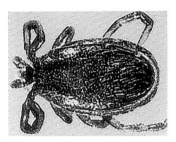

Adult fleas live on the dog but their eggs drop off the dog into the environment. There they go through four larval stages before reaching adulthood, and thereby are able to jump back on the poor unsuspecting dog. The cycle resumes and takes between 21 to 28 days under ideal conditions.

Ticks have forever been a common parasite of both man and dog and have achieved new infamy with their transmission of Lyme disease.Courtesy of Virbac Laboratories, Inc., Fort Worth, Texas.

There are environmental products available that will kill both the adult fleas and the larvae.

Ticks

Ticks carry Rocky Mountain Spotted Fever, Lyme disease and can cause tick paralysis. They should be removed with tweezers, trying to pull out the head. The jaws carry disease. There is a tick preventive collar that does an excellent job. The ticks automatically back out on those dogs wearing collars.

Sarcoptic Mange

This is a mite that is difficult to find on skin scrapings. The pinnal reflex is a good indicator of this disease. Rub the ends of the pinna (ear) together and the dog will start scratching with his foot. Sarcoptes are highly contagious to other dogs and to humans although they do not live long on humans. They cause intense itching.

Demodectic Mange

This is a mite that is passed from the dam to her puppies. It affects youngsters age three to ten months. Diagnosis is confirmed by skin scraping. Small areas of alopecia around the eyes, lips and/or forelegs become visible. There is little itching unless there is a secondary bacterial infection. Some breeds are afflicted more than others.

Cheyletiella

This causes intense itching and is diagnosed by skin scraping. It lives in the outer layers of the skin of dogs, cats, rabbits and humans. Yellow-gray scales may be found on the back and the rump, top of the head and the nose.

TO BREED OR NOT TO BREED

More than likely your breeder has requested that you have your puppy neutered or spayed. Your breeder's request is based on what is healthiest for your dog and what is most beneficial for your breed. Experienced and conscientious breeders devote many years into developing a bloodline. In order to do this, he makes every effort to plan each breeding in regard to conformation, temperament and health. This type of breeder does his best to perform the necessary testing (i.e., OFA, CERF, testing for inherited blood disorders, thyroid, etc.). Testing is expensive and sometimes very disheartening when a favorite dog doesn't pass his health tests. The health history pertains not only to the breeding stock but to the immediate ancestors. Reputable breeders do not want their offspring to be bred indiscriminately. Therefore you may be asked to neuter or spay your puppy. Of course there is always the exception, and your breeder may agree to let you breed your dog under his direct supervision. This is an important concept. More and more effort is being made to breed healthier dogs.

Because reputable breeders do not want their offspring to be bred indiscriminately, you may be asked to neuter or spay your puppy.

Spay/Neuter

There are numerous benefits of performing this surgery at six months of age. Unspayed females are subject to mammary and ovarian cancer. In order to prevent mammary cancer she must be spayed prior to her first heat cycle. Later in life, an unspayed female may develop a pyometra (an infected uterus), which is definitely life threatening.

Spaying is performed under a general anesthetic and is easy on the young dog. As you might expect it is a little harder on the older dog, but that is no reason to deny her

the surgery. The surgery removes the ovaries and uterus. It is important to remove all the ovarian tissue. If some is left behind, she could remain attractive to males. In order to view the ovaries, a reasonably long incision is necessary. An ovariohysterectomy is considered major surgery.

Neutering the male at a young age will inhibit some characteristic male behavior that owners frown upon. I have found my boys will not hike their legs and mark territory if they are neutered at six months of age. Also neutering at a young age has hormonal benefits, lessening the chance of hormonal aggressiveness.

Surgery involves removing the testicles but leaving the scrotum. If there should be a retained testicle, then he definitely needs to be neutered before the age of two or three years. Retained testicles can develop into cancer. Unneutered males are at risk for testicular cancer, perineal fistulas, perianal tumors and fistulas and prostatic disease.

Intact males and females are prone to housebreaking accidents. Females urinate frequently before, during and after heat cycles, and males tend to mark territory if there is a female in heat. Males may show the same

For the safety of your own dog or bitch, spaying or neutering is very beneficial to its health, as the risk of cancer of the reproductive organs is eliminated.

If you decide to breed your female, you should not attempt this until at least her second or third heat. behavior if there is a visiting dog or guests.

Surgery involves a sterile operating procedure equivalent to human surgery. The incision site is shaved, surgically scrubbed and draped. The veterinarian wears a sterile surgical gown, cap, mask and gloves. Anesthesia should be monitored by a registered technician. It is customary for the veterinarian to recommend a pre-anesthetic blood screening, looking for metabolic problems and a ECG rhythm strip to check for normal heart function. Today anesthetics are equal to human anesthetics, which enables your dog to walk out of the clinic the same day as surgery.

Some folks worry about their dog's gaining weight after being neutered or spayed. This is usually not the case. It is true that some dogs may be less active so they could develop a problem, but my own dogs are just as active as they were before surgery. I have a hard time keeping weight on them. However, if your dog should begin to gain, then you need to decrease his food and see to it that he gets a little more exercise.

DENTAL CARE for Your Dog's Life

So you've got a new puppy! You also have a new set of puppy teeth in your household. Anyone who has ever raised a puppy is abundantly aware of these new teeth. Your puppy will chew anything it can reach, chase your shoelaces, and play "tear the rag" with any piece of clothing it can find. When puppies are newly born, they have no teeth. At about four weeks of age, puppies of most breeds begin to develop their deciduous or baby teeth. They begin eating semi-solid food, fighting and biting with their litter mates, and learning discipline from their mother. As their new teeth come in, they inflict more pain on their mother's breasts, so her feeding sessions become less frequent and shorter. By six or eight weeks, the mother will start growling to warn her pups when they are fighting too roughly or hurting her as they nurse too much with their new teeth.

Puppies need to chew. It is a necessary part of their physical and mental development. They develop muscles and necessary life skills as they drag objects around, fight over possession, and vocalize alerts and warnings. Puppies chew on things to explore their world. They are using their sense of taste to determine what is food and what is not. How else can they tell an electrical cord from a lizard? At about four months of age, most puppies begin shedding their baby teeth.

All puppies need to chew; it is part of their physical and mental development. To appease this need, supply your puppy with plenty of safe chew devices from Nylabone®.

Often these teeth need some help to come out and make way for the permanent teeth. The incisors (front teeth) will be replaced first. Then, the adult canine or fang teeth erupt. When the baby tooth is not shed before the permanent tooth comes in, veterinarians call it a retained deciduous tooth. This condition will often cause gum infections by trapping hair and debris between the permanent tooth and the retained baby tooth. Nylafloss® is an excellent device for puppies to use. They can toss it, drag it, and chew on the many surfaces it presents. The baby teeth can catch in the nylon material, aiding in their removal. Puppies that have adequate chew toys will have less destructive behavior, develop more physically, and have less chance of retained deciduous teeth.

A chicken flavored Gumabone® has tiny particles of chicken powder embedded in it to keep your Rottweiler interested.

To avoid the build up of plaque, periodically check your dog's teeth and supply him with plenty of Nylabone® products.

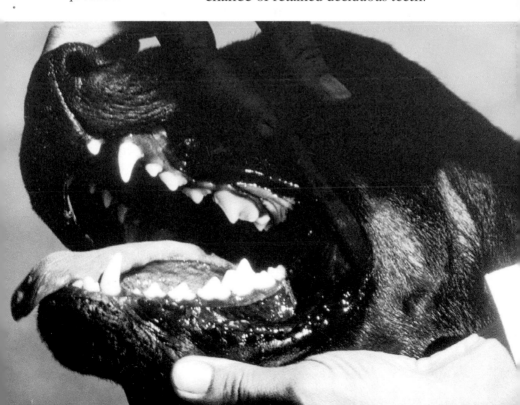

During the first year, your dog should be seen by your veterinarian at regular intervals. Your veterinarian will let you know when to bring in your puppy for vaccinations and parasite examinations. At each visit, your veterinarian should inspect the lips, teeth, and mouth as part of a complete physical examination. You should take some part in the maintenance of your dog's oral health. You should examine your dog's mouth weekly throughout his first year to make sure there are no sores, foreign objects, tooth problems, etc. If your dog drools excessively, shakes its head, or has bad breath, consult your veterinarian. By the time your dog is six months old, the permanent teeth are all in and plaque can start to accumulate on the tooth surfaces. This is when your dog needs to develop good dental-care habits to prevent calculus build-up on its teeth. Brushing is best. That is a fact that cannot be denied. However, some dogs do not like their teeth brushed regularly, or you may not be able to accomplish the task. In that case, you should consider a product that will help prevent plaque and calculus build-up.

The Plaque Attackers® and Galileo Bone® are other excellent choices for the first three years of a dog's life. Their shapes make them interesting for the dog. As the dog chews on them, the solid polyurethane massages the gums which improves the blood circulation to the periodontal tissues. Projections on the chew devices increase the surface and are in contact with the tooth for more efficient cleaning. The unique shape and consistency prevent your dog from exerting excessive force on his own teeth or from breaking off pieces of the bone. If your dog is an aggressive chewer or weighs more than 55 pounds (25 kg), you should consider giving him a Nylabone®, the most durable chew product on the market.

The Gumabone®, made by the Nylabone Company, is constructed of strong polyurethane, which is softer than nylon. Less powerful chewers prefer the Gumabones® to the Nylabones®. A super option your dog is the Hercules Bone®, a uniquely shaped bone named after the great Olympian for its exceptional strength. Like all Nylabone products, they are specially scented to make them attractive to your dog. Ask your veterinarian about these bones and he will validate the good doctor's prescription: Nylabones® not only give your dog a good chewing workout but also help to save your dog's teeth (and even his life, as it protects him from possible fatal periodontal diseases).

By the time dogs are four years old, 75% of them have periodontal disease. It is the most common infection in dogs. Yearly examinations by your veterinarian are essential to maintaining your dog's good health. If your veterinarian detects periodontal disease, he or she may recommend a prophylactic cleaning. To do a thorough cleaning, it will be necessary to put your dog under anesthesia. With modern gas anesthetics and monitoring equipment, the procedure is pretty safe. Your veterinarian will scale the teeth with an ultrasound scaler or hand instrument. This removes the calculus from the teeth. If there are calculus deposits below the gum line, the veterinarian will plane the roots to make them smooth. After all of the calculus has been removed, the teeth are polished with pumice in a polishing cup. If any medical or surgical treatment is needed, it is done at this time. The final step would be fluoride treatment and your follow-up treatment at home. If the periodontal disease is advanced, the veterinarian may prescribe a mediated mouth rinse or antibiotics for use at home. Make sure your dog has safe, clean and attractive chew toys and treats. Chooz® treats are another way of using a consumable treat to help keep your dog's teeth clean.

Molded rawhide, called Roar-Hide™ by Nylabone®, is very hard and safe for your dog. It is eagerly accepted by Rottweilers.

Rawhide is the most popular of all materials for a dog to chew. This has never been good news to dog owners, because rawhide is inherently very dangerous for dogs. Thousands of dogs have died from rawhide, having swallowed the hide after it has become soft and mushy, only to cause stomach and intestinal blockage. A new rawhide product on the market has finally solved the problem of rawhide: molded Roar-Hide® from Nylabone. These are composed of processed, cut up, and melted American rawhide injected into your dog's favorite shape: a dog bone. These dog-safe devices smell and taste like rawhide but don't break up. The ridges on the bones help to fight tartar build-up on the teeth and they last ten times longer than the usual rawhide chews.

As your dog ages, professional examination and cleaning should become more frequent. The mouth should be inspected at least once a year. Your veterinarian may recommend visits every six months. In the geriatric patient, organs such as the heart, liver, and kidneys do not function as well as when they were young. Your veterinarian will probably want to test these organs' functions prior to using general anesthesia for dental cleaning. If your dog is a good chewer and you work closely with your veterinarian, your dog can keep all of its teeth all of its life. However, as your dog ages, his sense of smell, sight, and taste will diminish. He may not have the desire to chase, trap or chew

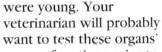

The Hercules® has been designed with Rottweilers and other large breeds in mind.

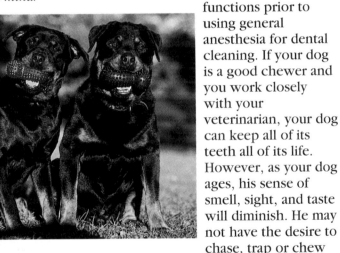

his toys. He will also not have the energy to chew for long periods, as arthritis and periodontal disease make chewing painful. This will leave you with more responsibility for keeping his teeth clean and healthy. The dog that would not let you brush his teeth at one year of age, may let you brush his teeth now that he is ten years old.

If you train your dog with good chewing habits as a puppy, he will have healthier teeth throughout his life.

Suggested Reading

TS-252
*Dog Behavior
and Training*

TS-249
*Skin & Coat Care
for Your Dog*

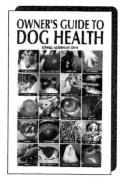

TS-214
*Owner's Guide
to Dog Health*

H-1083
*The World
of
Rottweilers*

TS-202
*The New
Rottweiler*

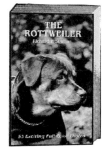

TS-147
*The Professional's
Book of Rottweilers*

PS-820
The Rottweiler

TW-142
*The Proper Care
of Rottweilers*

INDEX